SOUTH FROM
CHESTERFIELD CENTRAL

THE 'DERBYSHIRE LINES' OF THE
MANCHESTER, SHEFFIELD & LINCOLNSHIRE RAILWAY
– PART TWO A –

COMPILED AND WRITTEN BY

KEN GRAINGER

Published by Book Law Publications
382 Carlton Hill
Nottingham NG4 1JA

ISBN 978-1-909625-10-5

Printed by
The Amadeus Press
Cleckheaton, West Yorkshire, BD19 4TQ

INTRODUCTION

There had been great enthusiasm in Chesterfield when the Manchester, Sheffield & Lincolnshire Railway projected its Derbyshire Lines. The locals, convinced that the Midland Railway was abusing its monopoly in the town by overcharging its customers, welcomed the prospect of competition from a second railway company with open arms.

As described in 'Derbyshire Lines Part 1', the line from Sheffield Victoria via Beighton through to Chesterfield fully opened on June 4th, 1892. The contract for the Derbyshire Lines, amounting to £225,820, had been placed with Logan and Hemingway in January, 1890, but only one month later Baldry and Young had been handed responsibility for the construction of the final ten miles between Heath and Annesley and as early as January, 1892 Charles Liddell, engineer for the Derbyshire Lines, had reported that progress on the direct line onwards from Staveley towards Annesley was quite advanced despite snow and frost having caused considerable delays to brickwork and ironwork. Springwood tunnel, he advised, was complete "all except the front" (presumably the portals) "and only 180 of Annesley tunnel's 1,000 yards remained to be excavated", which he expected to be finished within four months. Also by the end of May, subject to land acquisition, he expected the deep cutting at Tibshelf to have been completed, where the ground had proved to be too unstable for the projected tunnel. The all-important colliery connections were proceeding apace too, those to Tibshelf and Pilsley, and to the Markham, Ireland and St. Johns collieries from Staveley progressing as rapidly as possible, though those to Holmewood and New Hucknall (confusingly, halfway between Tibshelf Town and Kirkby & Pinxton) were being held up by the Midland Railway's intransigence.

By September, 1892, Board of Trade inspection of the Staveley – Annesley line had been requested, and from October 24th MS&L goods trains were running over the line and, by the exercising of grudgingly granted running powers, over the Great Northern into Nottingham. The L&NW lost no time in exercising its own running powers over the new route, its own goods trains from Colwick into Sheffield beginning on December 5th, though it would still be more than two years before their own

Sheffield 'City Goods' depot was established, accessed via a branch off the MS&L main line at Woodburn Junction. The Great Northern did not exercise its reciprocal running powers over the new lines until after the Annesley extension opened to passenger traffic from January 2nd, 1893, including intermediate stations at Heath, Pilsley, Tibshelf Town and Kirkby & Pinxton, as it was originally known – renamed Kirkby Bentinck by the LNER from March 1st, 1925.

Chesterfield's enthusiasm for its new railway connection had, though, become quite muted when the penny dropped that Chesterfield was only being served by a terminal branch, the Derbyshire Lines' main line continuing straight-on from Staveley to meet the Great Northern at Annesley. Dismayed at being left out on a limb, the businessmen of Chesterfield immediately set about lobbying the MS&L to extend the Chesterfield branch southwards and complete a loop – a suggestion with which the MS&L complied with such alacrity (obtaining its Act for a 4¾ mile extension from Chesterfield to a junction with the main line just north of Heath on May 9th, 1890) that one might think it had been intended all along had its alignment not been so troublesome, including commencement via a tunnel under Chesterfield followed by a tortuous climb right up to Heath Junction.

Work on the Chesterfield – Heath section had progressed in parallel with the Annesley line, and it was ready for opening only six months afterwards, on July 3rd, 1893. The only station on the Chesterfield – Heath section, at Grassmoor, opened on November 1st, 1893.

There would still be further developments, such as overcoming Great Northern and L&NW objections (on whatever grounds, one wonders, where neither had any interest or access) to build the Williamthorpe colliery branch in 1906, and still to come were the 1907 connections to the newly acquired LD&EC but to all intents and purposes the MS&L Derbyshire Lines were complete. Not, of course, that Sir Edward Watkin would be allowing anyone to rest on their laurels........

ACKNOWLEDGEMENTS

This is the part of a book which, it would appear, most tends to be overlooked: I hope it won't be in this case because there are many people who deserve recognition for making it possible. First of all must be David Allen of Book Law Publications, who made the initial approach for the writing of the book, or rather books, since the wealth of material needed an extension into a second volume. His enthusiasm and encouragement has been instrumental throughout the preparation. The late Greg Fox, though, must also be acknowledged: he published The MS&L Derbyshire Lines Part One: Sheffield Victoria to Chesterfield Central, and provided the 'Scenes from the Past' format, the lasting inspiration and blueprint for railway line surveys.

And then there are those who provided the material. The beautiful and evocative painting on the cover, an everyday scene in the late 'fifties of D11 *Gerard Powys Dewhurst* at Chesterfield Central, is by courtesy of David Charlesworth GRA, and the 'First Sod Turning' programme, also very artistic, is from the beautiful original in Alan Rowles' collection. Of the photographs, wherever possible individual photographers are credited, and thank goodness so many expert photographers thought to record the line before it passed into history. Some amongst them deserve a special mention: Syd Hancock combined photographic expertise with an ability to find locations which nobody else knew of, and Michael Mensing who remarkably only visited the Derbyshire Lines once, but what photographs he took back home with him ! Then there is John Hitchens who, as well as some fine photographs, gave unstintingly of his expert knowledge of his Kirkby-in-Ashfield stamping ground, and coverage of New Hucknall Sidings would be bleak indeed without David Dykes' contribution. There is a brief introduction here to the the Railway Correspondence and Travel Society's Courtney Haydon collection, for allowing selection from which special thanks are due to Cyril Crawley. The Courtney Haydon collection though assumes paramount importance in the portraying of the so very neglected territory south of Annesley.

Individual locomotive detail which adds so much to the story has been gleaned from various volumes of 'Yeadon's Register of LNER Locomotives' and from numerous issues of 'Locomotives Illustrated', but the book is essentially about the railway, portrayed in the fine maps and track diagrams prepared by Andrew Crawford of Amadeus Press, from beautiful but fragile MS&L originals.

In addition to allowing selection from his photographic collection, Richard Morton has painstakingly proofread the manuscript, adding a consummate depth of knowledge of railways in general and the Great Central in particular to his fine command of the so frequently abused English language – nevertheless it goes without saying that even if note had been taken of all his recommendations, responsibility for the inevitable errors, not to mention personal opinions, rests entirely with the author.

Finally, the family. I must thank my brother, David, not just for his considerable help and encouragement with this book (he knows a darn sight more than I about the modern railway) but for first kindling a lifetime's interest in railways, even if I never did quite get into the trainspotting thing. And last but very definitely not least, my wife Carol, for her boundless tolerance of my railway interest, this "phase I am going through", for her constant encouragement in getting on with the book(s), and for putting up with that heap of photographs, documents, maps, books and goodness knows what else behind the settee !

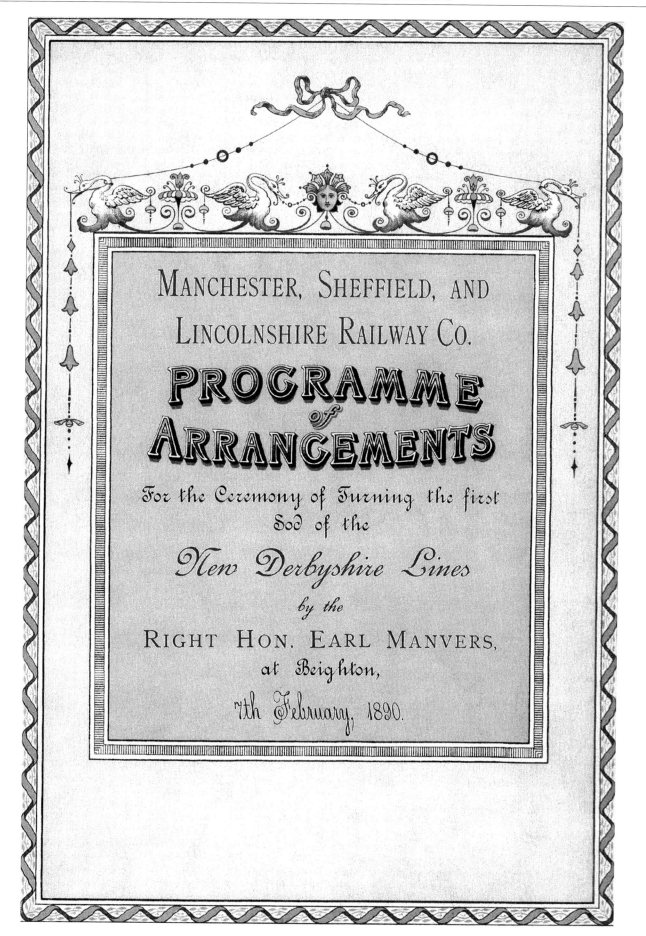

MANCHESTER, SHEFFIELD, AND LINCOLNSHIRE RAILWAY CO.

PROGRAMME *of* ARRANGEMENTS

For the Ceremony of Turning the first Sod of the

New Derbyshire Lines

by the

RIGHT HON. EARL MANVERS,

at Beighton,

7th February, 1890.

The invited Guests will assemble between noon and half-past twelve o'clock, on the site where the Ceremony is to take place, which closely adjoins the Beighton Station on the Company's Eckington Branch.

THE CEREMONY OF TURNING THE FIRST SOD,
BY

THE RIGHT HONOURABLE EARL MANVERS,

will be performed at 12-30 p.m.

After short Addresses, the guests will proceed by Special Train to Sheffield, where LUNCHEON will be provided in the Company's Royal Victoria Station Hotel, at 1-30 p.m.

For the convenience of Visitors, the following TRAIN ARRANGEMENTS have been made :—

A Special Train will leave

	a.m.
Manchester (London Road) at	10 40
Calling at Mottram ... ... „	10 56
Hadfield ... ... „	11 2
Wortley ... ... „	11 34
Sheffield ... ... arr. „	11 50
„ ... ... dep. „	12 5
Arriving at Beighton ... ... „	12 20

The LUNCHEON TRAIN will leave Beighton Station at 12-50 p.m., and reach Sheffield Station at 1-5 p.m.

The Return Special Train will leave

	p.m.
Sheffield ... ... at	3 45
Calling at Wortley	4 0
Hadfield... ... ... „	4 32
Mottram ... ... „	4 38
Arriving at Manchester (London Road) „	4 55

The presentation of the Invitation Card will Pass the holder Free by the Special Trains above named, or by any Ordinary Train over the Company's System.

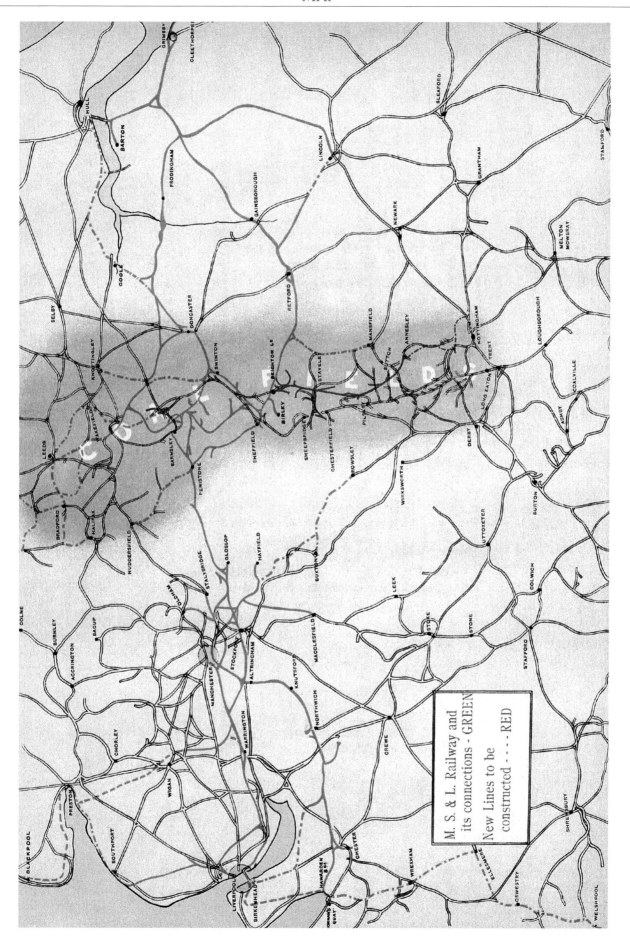

M. S. & L. Railway and
its connections - GREEN

New Lines to be
constructed - - - - RED

CHESTERFIELD TO HEATH

'Derbyshire Lines Part 1' brought us as far as Chesterfield Central and that is where we shall resume our journey, again in the company of the LNER's official photographer, though we can wish that he had chosen a better day than the dismal and slushy January 23rd, 1936 to make his visit. As has already been noted Chesterfield Central changed little over the years, and its frontage not at all, other than the proclamation of its successive owners. By 1936 that was, of course, the London & North Eastern Railway, in full, which required the full width of the canopy.   *LNER Official*

As may be seen, the final version nameboard – and this is at the time of closure - also extended across the full width of the canopy but only to include a couple of British Railways totems on the Eastern Region blue enamel. The building was very presentable right to the end in cream and green. The crane visible on the left was engaged in the building of Chesterfield's Technical College extension, which would dwarf the original flat roofed building beyond.

Reverting to those LNER officials of January 23rd, 1936, we have now come through the entrance (to the right of the photographer) and entered the booking hall, where we can admire the underside of the French Empire style roof. The hanging gas light will be noted, and the two ticket windows. Latterly, sadly, just the further one was more than sufficient.

LNER Official

Through the booking hall, a transverse corridor (see Derbyshire Lines Pt 1 page 140) gave access to the stairways down to the platforms: this is to the Up (southbound) platform.

LNER Official

Having descended the stairs we are now looking northwards along Chesterfield Central's Up platform. It has to be admitted that the platform buildings look distinctly dingy despite the best attempts of the LNER headed poster and timetable displays. It would all have been so much brighter when the canopies were fully glazed gables, before the sloping of the outer section and the replacement of two-thirds of the glazing by utilitarian corrugated asbestos. Perhaps the "Liverpool Overhead" poster might have been more pertinent on the Down platform ?   *LNER Official*

A look across to the Up platform from the northern end of the Down platform, most unusually for a southerly view omitting Chesterfield parish church's 'crooked spire' (just out of shot to the right). That miniature spire on the skyline above the station is part of the Stephenson Memorial Hall, which nowadays houses the Pomegranite Theatre and Chesterfield Museum. Not infrequently the centre road would be occupied by a couple of spare carriages, available for the reinforcement of overfilled trains. What a quaint practice that now seems ! The date is indeterminate: the running in board is original but wasn't re-placed by an enamel one until the late 'fifties. Trebor Sweets have taken over and begun to expand the former Chesterfield Brewery premises. They would later be surrounded by flat-roofed extensions but now, of course, like the railway, its all gone.   *E.M.Johnson collection*

Another of Chesterfield Central's stalwarts, Bob Dukeson, regards the photographer utilising the signal box vantage point to record a Great Central locomotive type not often seen on the Derbyshire Lines, the A5. No 69803 is either stabling or retrieving a duo of Gresley articulated twins in the centre road, against a backdrop of Chesterfield Royal Hospital's nurses home and Brewery Street's terraced cottages. During Great Central days, Robinson's admirable class 9N 'Coronation Tanks' all resided at Neasden, where they had displaced the 9K and 9L Atlantic tanks and established a mastery of the Marylebone outer suburbans which they wouldn't relinquish for little short of forty years – indeed the last ones didn't follow their sisters northwards until 1954. The 'Coronation Tanks' owed their nickname to their introduction having coincided with the coronation of King George V and Queen Mary, and no. 69803 (as GC no. 168) was amongst the earliest, in May 1911. Their eventual dispersal included allocations to the Manchester, Nottingham and West Riding areas, but not to Sheffield. However, history has repeated itself and 69803, lately of Boston has again displaced Atlantic tanks, this time at Staveley, but not for long. She will in her turn be replaced by the return of the 'Directors', finally becoming surplus to requirements at Lincoln in June, 1959. *Graham Perrin collection*

The A5s had initially been replaced at Neasden by Edward Thompson's L1 2-6-4 tanks – where they were nick named 'Concrete Mixers', absolutely hated, and moved on as quickly as possible ! A major moan at Neasden was the draughtiness of their cabs, but they were known for "rattling themselves to bits" and springing leaks in their tanks, and it is undeniable that they had an inordinate attraction to shops. Apparently they were much better appreciated at Colwick where, however, they were not replacing more solidly built Great Central engines ! Robert Stephenson and Hawthorn built no 67800 was the last of the class, not entering traffic until September, 1950 and spending her whole life on the former Great Northern, at Kings Cross and Grantham before finally arriving at Colwick in April, 1962. Liked or not, she was withdrawn from there that December, but in the meantime is showing off her electric lights (the Stone's steam turbine is visible on the right hand side of the running plate) as she arrives at Chesterfield Central on a dismal May 19th with the 10.18 am Sheffield Victoria – Nottingham Victoria 'stopper'. She is just passing Chesterfield Central's signal box, like all those originally provided on the Derbyshire Lines, of the standard MS&L/Great Central type 3. Behind the box what looks to be an O1 is lurking, though it could be an O4/8, and looming in the murk beyond is the goods warehouse. Of the contraption on the left, the less said the better ! *A. Moyes*

Left: This is one third of the new loading/unloading facilities. Just take a quick look, shudder, and move on.

Below: A closer look at the goods warehouse. The newer brickwork to the left of the office extension reveals how the original through road for loading and unloading purposes has been replaced by the knocking through of three windows, the apertures then having been given protection from the elements by primitive corrugated iron hoods. Goodness knows why the extra storage space was required but the alteration could hardly have been more crudely effected.

Graham Perrin collection

A busy scene in the goods yard with the warehouse proudly proclaiming its ownership, and a reminder of that now far-off era when local businesses looked exclusively to the railway for anything other than local carriage. Even so, obviously the consignment of 25 tons of confectionery on behalf of S. Elliott, of Steeple Works, Park Road, Chesterfield was something quite out of the ordinary. Presumably that is the proprietor, beside the station master at centre left. The two gentlemen second and third from left look quite important too and the carters all look rather spruce with even the horses seeming conscious of the camera.

Back to the passenger station (and to the BR era) just in time for the arrival of another up 'stopper', behind an ex-Great Northern K2 'Ragtimer' – so named by GC men for their pronounced rocking and rolling - not an uncommon type around the Chesterfield loop. Her smokebox number looks to be 61767 (GN class H3 no. 1677, North British Loco., August 1918) which isn't unlikely, she was latterly a Colwick engine before her January 1961 withdrawal.

Graham Perrin collection

Chesterfield Central's Up platform as it would have been seen from the K2's footplate. The foot of the stairs down from the booking hall is visible at the far end of the platform, beyond the ubiquitous stove-enamelled advertisements including such ever-presents as Virol; Palethorpes Sausages; Bryant and May Matches; Suttons Seeds and Camp Coffee. Looking beneath the booking hall on its Infirmary Road overbridge, Brewery Street bridge is visible and immediately beyond as the line veers to the left, the right hand edge of Chesterfield Tunnel's north portal. An immediate consequence of the second thought continuation of the Chesterfield branch, to form a loop, was that the line had to burrow under the promontory on which the town stood, before tackling a vicious climb to rejoin the main line at Heath. *LNER Official*

Railway Preservation Society

Great Central Railway

COMMEMORATIVE TRIP

TO LONDON (Marylebone) & RETURN

including 4 hours in London

SATURDAY, JUNE 15TH

SPECIAL TRAIN OF EX-LNER STOCK

HAULED BY

LNER A3 PACIFIC
"FLYING SCOTSMAN"

Departs Sheffield Victoria 8-50 a.m.
Arrive back ,,   ,,   9-42 p.m.

Refreshment Car facilities.   Stops at points of interest en route

---

FARE 45/- RETURN

Tickets from : RAILWAY PRESERVATION SOCIETY
24 CHORLEY DRIVE, SHEFFIELD 10.
Tel. 31072

The renowned *Flying Scotsman* emerging from the south portal of the 474 yards long Chesterfield tunnel, overlooked by Hollis Lane. Its northerly approach and the site of Chesterfield Central station have been usurped for Chesterfield's 'Inner Relief Road' (sounds for all the world like a laxative, doesn't it ?) but then the road swings sharply to the east, alongside the retaining wall which hides the sealed off northern portal of Chesterfield tunnel. Nowadays, looking northwards from truncated Hollis Lane, what many presume to be the fenced off southern portal can be seen, a blue brick arch shrouded in concrete. It is not though the tunnel portal. Chesterfield tunnel was only partially a true tunnel, which ended with a ventilation shaft adjacent to Spa Lane; it is the wall of that which is still visible. The tunnel was then continued by cut-and-cover to the tunnel mouth seen in Graham Perrin's photograph. This, though, is a remarkable photograph: Chesterfield Central and the loop had closed to passengers on March 4th, 1963, but here, over three months later *Flying Scotsman* (at that time owned by Alan Pegler) is heading a special traversing the loop, including a call at Chesterfield Central, which would surely be unthinkable today. It is the Railway Preservation Society's June 15th, 1963 Great Central Commemorative Special, which set out from Sheffield Victoria at 8.50 am. It must now be about 9.30, give or take a couple of minutes, as she was due to arrive at Chesterfield Central at 9.23 and depart at 9.26. After calling at "points of interest" en route she will be at Marylebone by 1.25 pm, to give her complement 4 hours in London and have them back at Sheffield Victoria for 9.42 pm – but this time straight up the main line rather than via the Chesterfield loop. Not a bad day out for £2.25 return, was it ? *Graham Perrin*

A 'double-header' hurrying away from the Chesterfield tunnel, with B1 4-6-0 no. 61138 piloting the last L1 2-6-4 tank, no. 67800, which we have already met arriving at Chesterfield Central on another up 'stopper'. They have just pulled out of Chesterfield Central with the 11.07 am departure for Nottingham Victoria on what was obviously a bone chillingly cold December 29th, 1962. The building above and to the left of the train, with the semi-hipped roof, was formerly the Central station master's house. The Chesterfield loop has but a couple of months left (the "Hillman Super Minx" billboard hints strongly at the in vogue form of transport). No. 61138 will last somewhat longer, until January 1965 – still a tragically short life with her only having emerged from North British Loco's Queen's Park Works in March, 1947 - but for Colwick's no. 67800 this will be her final journey, until she is dragged off to Darlington for breaking up.

Geoff Newall

Very shortly after her June, 1962 emergence from Vulcan Foundry and allocation to Darnall, what we then knew as English Electric Type 3 no. D6742 is getting away from Chesterfield with the 4.10 pm Sheffield Victoria – Nottingham Victoria, alongside the billboards facing onto Lordsmill Street. Such workings as this were never usual though, neither the Chesterfield loop or, for that matter, the Great Central main line were ever really dieselised. D6742 is still around, preserved as Class 37 no. 37042 at the formative Eden Valley Railway, Warcop, long after the Chesterfield loop and, for that matter, Darnall Shed have been consigned to history. The girder bridge under which D6742 has just passed carries the former Midland Railway's Brampton goods branch, which continues westwards over Lordsmill Street, then Chesterfield's southward road exit, beside the Hillman Super Minx advert.

J. Phipps

The two preceding photographs were taken from the footbridge seen here, familiar to a generation of Chesterfield 'loco-spotters' as "the Forty Steps" and invaluable for commanding views of both the Great Central loop and the much busier Midland main line, from where these photographs were taken. It would also have given sight of trains passing over the one-time Lancashire, Derbyshire and East Coast line into Chesterfield Market Place station, but they were long gone by now. The large building in the right background is the old silk mill, latterly Harrisons Boot and Shoe factory, which was demolished in 1967. It was no great loss architecturally. Lordsmill Street and the Great Central and Midland lines are each bridging the River Hipper, a west-to-east flowing tributary of the River Rother which it will join just a few yards behind the photographer. Noticeably the Great Central tracks are parting to pass either side of the central pier of the obliquely angled bridge underneath the Midland line.

D.Ibbotson, by courtesy of E.M.Johnson

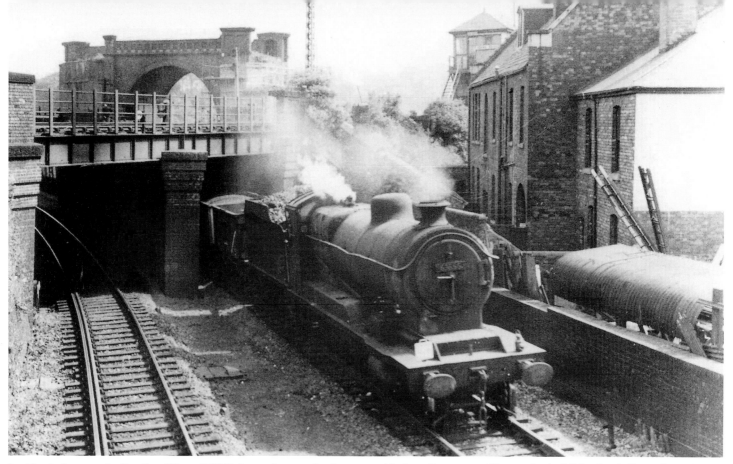

Looking in the opposite direction, O4 no. 63656 brings a down coal train, presumably from Grassmoor colliery, under the Midland main line and past the rear of the Horns Hotel, which is partly masking the Midland's Horns Bridge signal box. She has also just passed under the remains of the Lancashire, Derbyshire and East Coast Railway's Horns Bridge viaduct, the steel spans of which were dismantled in 1960. The absence of a vacuum brake pipe from 63656's buffer beam identify her as an ex-ROD O4/3 (ROD no. 1617, built by Kitsons in June, 1918) and she's been around. After returning from France in December 1919, she went on loan to the Great Western Railway, their No. 3068, until June 1922 when she was returned and stored at the Beachley dump, near Chepstow. She was finally purchased by the LNER in December, 1923 but will not outlast the Chesterfield loop, withdrawal coming in December, 1962.   *G.Newall*

The same scene in the Edwardian era. There are few differences, though they were happier days for the LD&ECR at least. Shirebrook coal is trundling northwards on the Midland, having just come under the bowstring girder section of the LD&EC viaduct, which is being crossed by a Chesterfield Market Place – Lincoln Central train behind a bunker-first class C 0-4-4 tank. She is just about to pass over the Chesterfield loop line, which curves under the centre one of the three reinforced plate-girder spans. The LD&EC's self-styled "DUKERIES ROUTE" soubriquet will be noted on the parapet of the masonry arch. It seems incredible that virtually no sign of the viaduct remains today, only a block of blue brick, the foot of the one-time Derby Road arch, propping up the Midland line embankment. Not the most successful of the LD&EC's engines (they were somewhat undersized), all six of the C class were withdrawn as the LNER's class G3 between 1931 and 1935.   *Nadin's postcard*

Overlooked by the Midland's Horns Bridge signal box, K3 no. 61808 has brought the 10.42 Sheffield Victoria – Nottingham Victoria 'stopper' under the Midland line (and another footbridge), with her fireman 'digging in' for the hard 1-in-80 slog up to Heath. K3s were known to GC enginemen as 'Jazzers', another jibe at the liveliness of Doncaster's locomotives, less solidly built than the "built like battleships" progeny of Gorton. No. 61808 was one of the original ten-strong Great Northern H4 class (GN no. 1008, Doncaster, July 1921) but is now in her final days. She will be withdrawn from Colwick in September 1961, to be followed by all of her sisters by the end of the following year. *Colin Walker*

B1 no. 61124 brings a down local through the remains of the LD&EC viaduct in 1961/2. The line to the left of the locomotive is the beginning of the gated Hydes sidings, which branched off the up main just beyond the viaduct and continued beyond Robert Hyde's foundry to serve the Clayton Street Tannery and Markham & Co's Broad Oaks works. The sidings continued in use for some time after the withdrawal of scheduled services, which may be why *Flying Scotsman's* June, 1963 passage of the loop line was possible. No. 61124 lasted until September, 1962, a mere 15 years after she had emerged from North British Loco's Queen's Park Works in February, 1947, but that was still longer than some of her classmates managed.
Graham Perrin

Turning the clock back to the 1950s we can see how Hydes Sidings were served. Someone from Chesterfield Central has ridden through the tunnel on the goods train's engine, with the requisite Annett's key from the Central signal box, to unlock the points and open the gate into the sidings. The goods brake has been uncoupled and left on the up line while the engine is about to back into the sidings and shunt as required. Passenger services along the former LD&EC line into Chesterfield Market Place station ceased from 1951 when the parlous state of subsidence-ravaged Bolsover tunnel and Carr Vale viaduct caused the line to be severed west of Langwith Junction. However, until 1957 Market Place continued to be served by a daily goods train, arriving from Staveley via the 1907 Duckmanton North Junction, and it is during this period that we see an unidentified 'Pom-Pom', having completed her shunting, heading back tender first to Staveley.

In another 1950s view, Stanier LMS 'Black Five' no. 45267 is powering away from Chesterfield. Black Fives were never a common type around the Chesterfield loop and in the 'fifties no. 45267 was a Kentish Town engine, but the express passenger lamp code suggests this might be a diversion, and engineer possessions of the pitfall-bedevilled main line were a frequent occurrence. On the other hand, some expresses were scheduled to traverse the loop with a Chesterfield stop. Getting a run at the stiff climb up to Heath made for spirited Up departures from Chesterfield: much of the line has now been usurped for the A617 dual carriageway and, even by road standards, the climb is noticeable. Ironically, no. 45267 (Armstrong Whitworth, October 1936) was to be one of the clapped-out Black Fives which saw out the 'Nottingham semi-fast' death throes of the Great Central main line in September 1966. She met her own end in October, 1967.

W. Wagstaffe

About three miles south-east of Chesterfield and at a brief easing of the gradient up to Heath, Grassmoor was the only station on the afterthought Chesterfield – Heath link completing the Chesterfield loop. Perhaps the station was itself an afterthought, not opening until November 1st, 1893, some months after the July 3rd opening of the line. That could go some way to explaining the one-off station design: built in a cutting, the station was of brick with its main, southbound building two-storeyed, the first floor being at road level and giving access to a footbridge with stairways down to both platforms. Grassmoor colliery, situated a little way south of the station, had already been operational before the coming of the railway, but its new railway outlet contributed to a rapid expansion working the profitable Blackshale seam. Grassmoor itself was the archetypal "pit village", the vast majority of its breadwinners being employed at the colliery, but obviously they cannot have provided enough patronage to make the station worthwhile. Even the exigencies of World War II could not dissuade the LNER from closing the station on October 28th, 1940. Grassmoor station seems to have been rather less than a mecca for railway photographers, but was still essentially intact when photographed in 1947. The view is looking south, and the lines visible on the right lead to the colliery.

Douglas Thompson

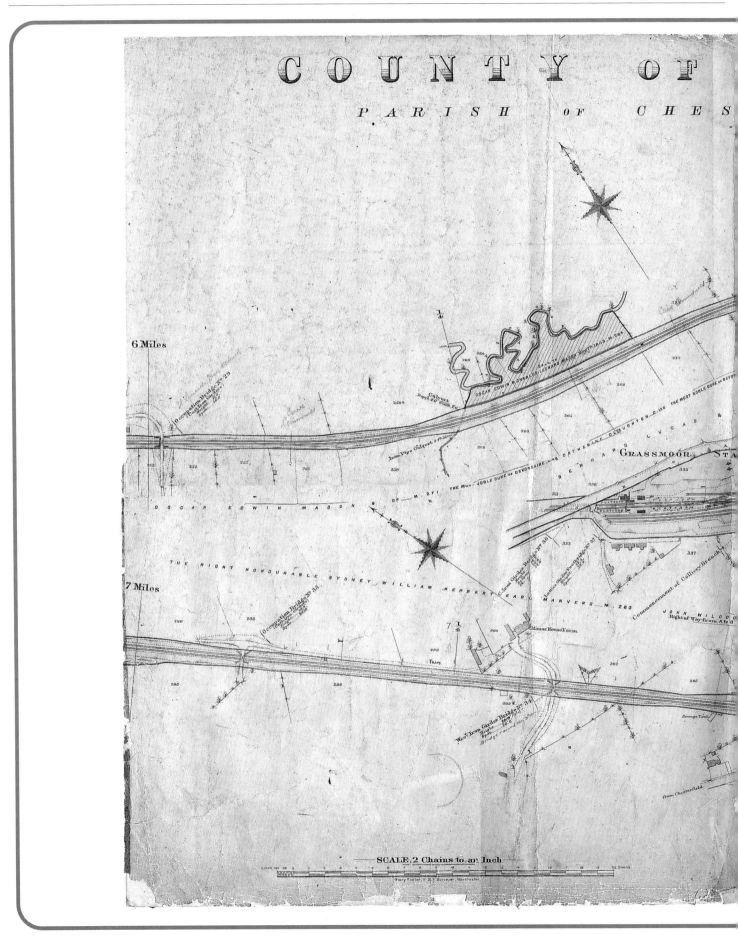

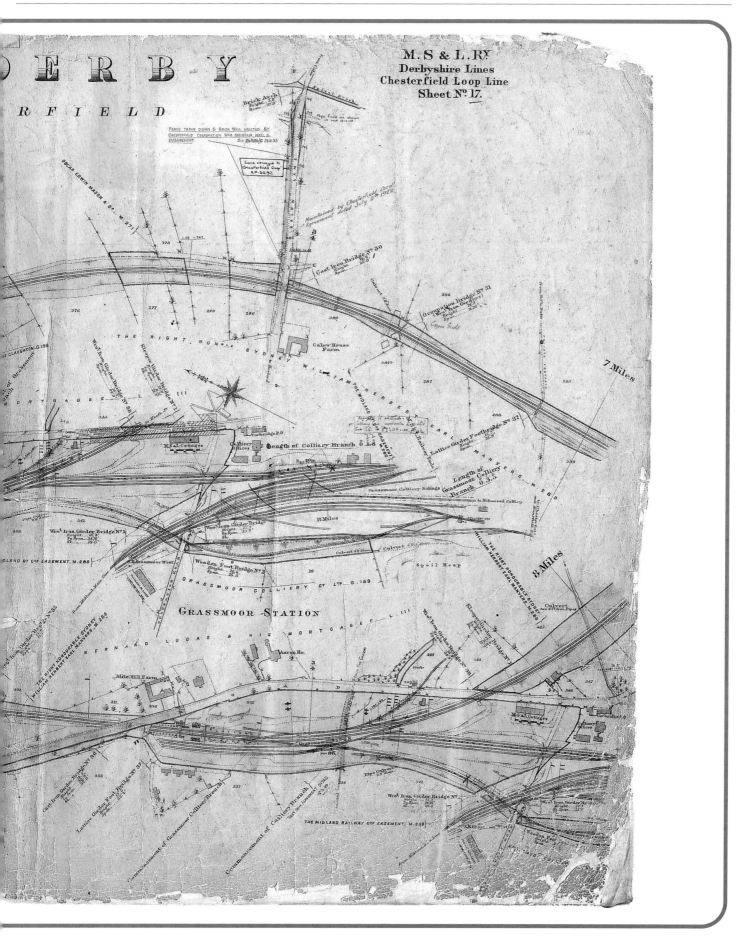

By July 1959 when Darnall's B1 no. 61111 (North British, December 1946) swept by with an 'all-stations' to Sheffield Victoria, Grassmoor station was slowly disappearing. Only the 'Gents', retained to serve permanent way staff, remains on the crumbling northbound platform. Grassmoor colliery is visible in the distance, still providing business for the railway and keeping the station signal box busy. The colliery would continue as a training centre until the late '80s, but ceased turning coal in 1967, some years after 61111's withdrawal in September, 1962.

H.B. Priestley

Perhaps Grassmoor station had one of its busier days on Saturday July 12th, 1913, when cheap tickets were on offer to Belle Vue for the annual brass band contest. A good take up must have been anticipated since passengers from Grassmoor (where the station was probably more convenient for Hasland than for its own village), Staveley and Woodhouse were directed to travel to Sheffield by an earlier train than those from Chesterfield and Renishaw. If the bands performed in the order given, the audience would have been sick and tired of the selection from Mozart's 'Don Giovanni' by the time they heard it for the fortieth time played by the Hasland band !

The Battle of Lule Burgas 'Grand Spectacle' might have come as a welcome change, the re-enactment of the October 30th – November 2nd 1912 rout of the Turks by a numerically weaker Bulgarian army in the largest European battle fought since the Franco-Prussian War. At the time it was regarded as a great slaughter but would pale by comparison with the looming Great War.

It was going to be a long and weary day, with the returning excursionists not setting out from Manchester London Road until 11.20 pm.

Michael Mensing only paid one visit to the Derbyshire Lines, on 29th September, 1959, but made good use of his visit. The furthest north he reached was Grassmoor Colliery, where he photographed Staveley Shed's J11 'Pom-Pom' no. 64444, at this point propelling loaded coal wagons towards the colliery. A notable engine, as the Great Central's No. 16, no. 64444 emerged from Gorton in April, 1909 as the Great Central's first superheated engine. The Great Central's classification was 9J but they were always and universally the 'Pom-Poms', so named by soldiers returning from South Africa, from the supposed similarity between the bark of their exhausts and the army's then new quick-firing gun. Originally fitted with piston valves, no. 64444 had been brought into line with her slide valve-fitted sisters in 1927, then finally had been one of the last rebuilt as a J11/3 with long-travel piston valves and a higher pitched boiler, in July 1947. As such she would soldier on until May, 1961.

Michael Mensing

A last look back at Grassmoor's signal box, soon after it had been repainted cream and green in 1959, and the crumbling remains of the station, before continuing up the bank to Heath. On the way, we shall pass Bonds Main Colliery, sunk from 1895 and producing top quality house coal from 1898 until it closed in 1953.

Lens of Sutton

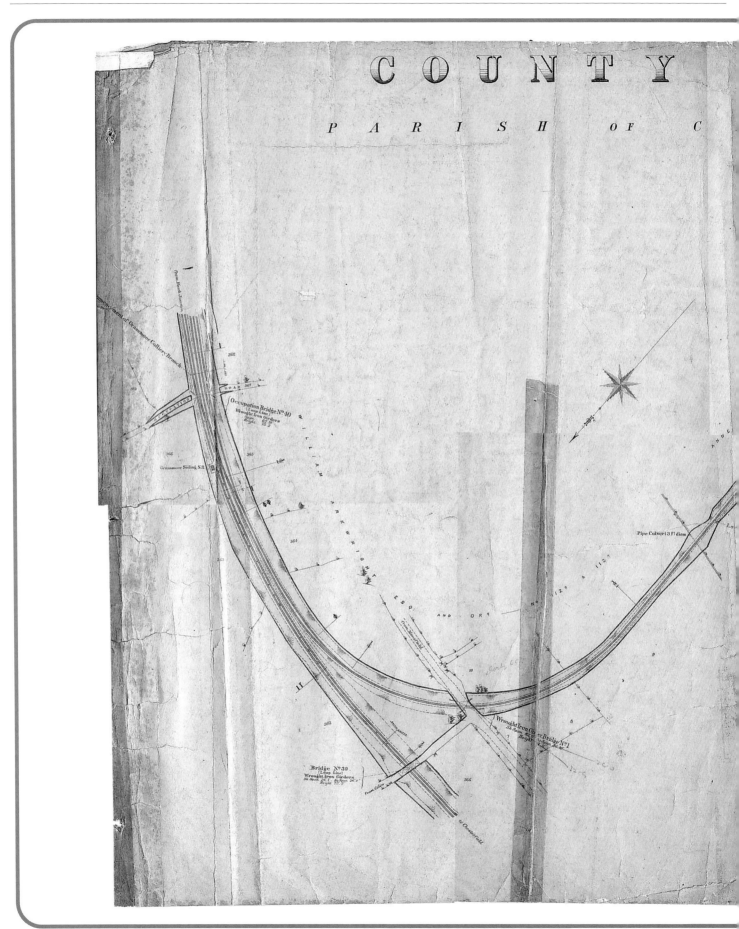

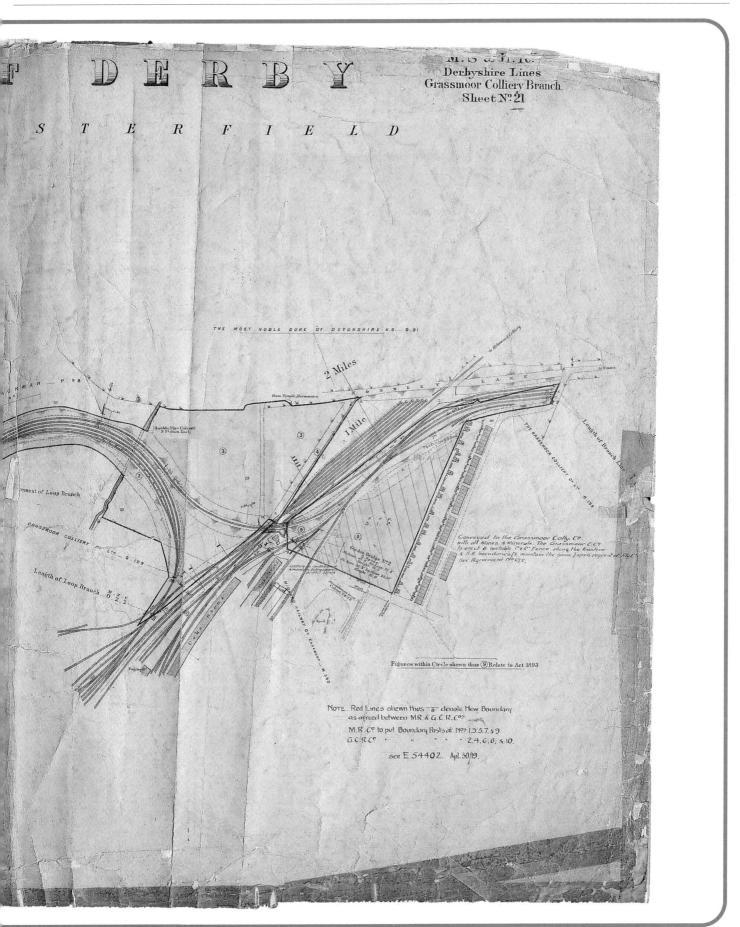

We're looking back northwards from Heath station's roadbridge to where the Chesterfield loop rejoined the main line at Heath Junction (beyond its signal box, in the left distance). Staveley's class O4/8 no. 63612 is shunting wagons for the Williamthorpe Colliery branch, which curves away to the right before swinging sharp left and passing under the main line adjacent to Heath Junction, immediately beyond the 'box. The railway's coming must have been instrumental in the sinking of Williamthorpe colliery, which commenced in 1901. By 1905 the deepest mine in the East Midlands was producing up to 4,000 tons of top quality house coal per day, again tapping into the Black Shale seam. Another prime source of energy which was wantonly discarded in 1970. No. 63612 entered service as Great Central class 8K no. 387 in January, 1914. She remained in her original form (LNER/BR class O4/1) until rebuilt with a 100A boiler as an O4/8 in July, 1955. Withdrawal came in November, 1965.

Bob Tebb

STAVELEY TO HEATH

'Derbyshire Lines Pt 1' came as far as Staveley Town (Staveley Central from 1950) then veered off westwards to Chesterfield. Loop line services used platforms 3 and 4, on the far side in this south looking view of the station. The main line platforms 1 and 2 continued straight on, straddled by the booking hall on the Worksop Road bridge. Photographs of Staveley Town with its original, gable ended platform canopies are extremely rare: as at many Derbyshire Lines stations, their outer ends were later lightened by bevelling to produce a hipped profile.

Immediately south of Staveley Central, looking down from the Worksop Road was Staveley South Junction, being passed by a latter-day Bournemouth – York behind a Tinsley class 47. To the right, the rusting rails and those wagons curving away to the west are what remains of the Chesterfield loop, closed since 1963. The wagons on the left are on the Markham Colliery branch, dividing the main line from the derelict Staveley Central shed which closed with the cessation of Great Central line through freights in June 1965, and will be demolished in 1967. In the left distance is the chimney of Ireland Colliery, formerly served by a branch line, the track bed of which can be seen skirting the backs of the MS&L built Railway Cottages. Nowadays known as "Belmont Drive", they are all that remains of this scene. ***RCTS/Courtney Haydon collection***

Looking back northwards at Staveley South Junction, the Worksop Road bridge is only vaguely visible through the exhaust of O1 no. 63594 at the head of a through goods, making an all-out charge at the Staveley Bank, eight miles of virtually unbroken 1-in-100 up to Heath and on to the summit at Pilsley. The lines veering away to the left of the signal box are the beginning of the Chesterfield loop, while to the right, between the main line and Staveley Central shed, is the Markham colliery branch, with offshoots along the way to St. John's Colliery and a second, southern access to Ireland Colliery. All, of course, are long gone, and it is hard nowadays to visualise just how completely the coal industry once dominated this area. As Great Central no. 333, 63594 had been amongst the earliest of the 8K 'Tinies', built at Gorton in November, 1911. In November 1947 she was rebuilt as an O1, one of 58 conversions, no less than 53 of which had been concentrated at Annesley for working the Woodford 'Runners'. After being displaced on those duties by the admirable BR Standard 9Fs, their subsequent dispersal included some to Staveley, where no. 63594 ended her days in April, 1964.

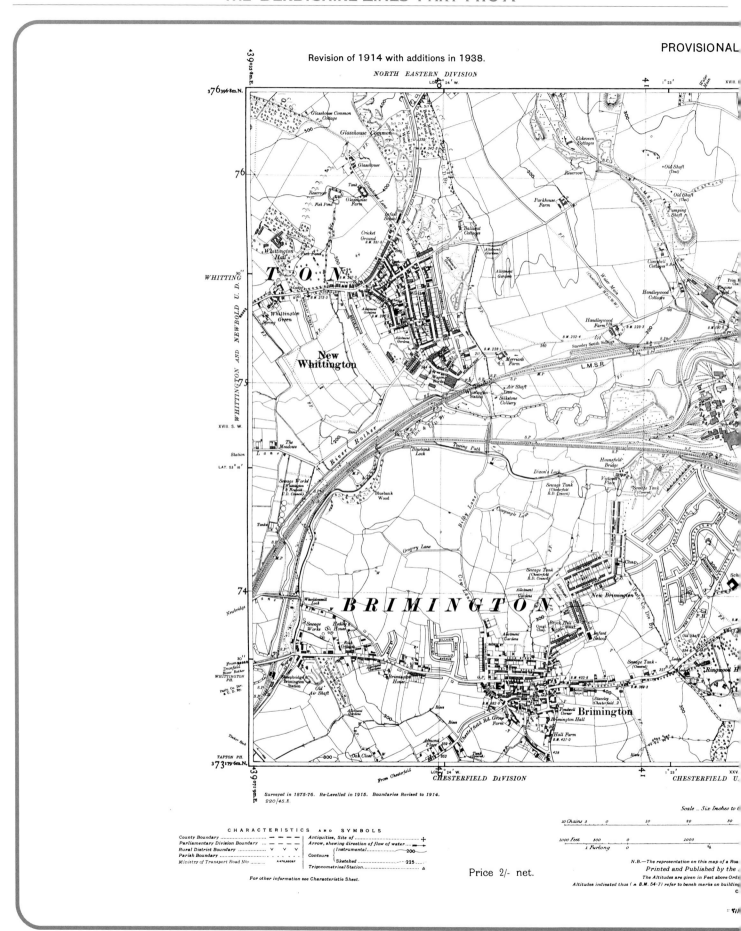

Revision of 1914 with additions in 1938.

PROVISIONAL

Price 2/- net.

Surveyed in 1875-76. Re-Levelled in 1915. Boundaries Revised to 1914.
220/45.E.

CHARACTERISTICS AND SYMBOLS

County Boundary .... — — —
Parliamentary Division Boundary ... — · — ·
Rural District Boundary .... v v v
Parish Boundary ....
Ministry of Transport Road Nos .... A A70,63087

Antiquities, Site of .... +
Arrow, shewing direction of flow of water ....
   Instrumental 200
Contours
   Sketched 225
Trigonometrical Station .... △

For other information see Characteristic Sheet.

O4/8 no. 63914 on the Markham Colliery branch, with what look to be oil tanks marshalled in with the usual mineral wagons. How much height the diverging main line, to the left, has already attained accentuates the steepness of the Staveley bank, beginning virtually from Staveley Central's platform ends. No. 63914 has seen some changes. Built as the Great Central Railway's no. 12 at Gorton in September, 1919, she was originally one of the GC's class 8M (LNER O5) with a 5'6" diameter boiler. All were subsequently rebuilt with standard O4 5' boilers, no. 12 (by then LNER no. 5012) in August 1926. In July 1955 she was finally rebuilt to O4/8, with a 100A boiler like the O1, but retaining her original cylinders and Stephenson valve gear, which would see her through to her May, 1964 demise.

Immediately beyond South Junction, to the west of the line, stood Speedwell Terrace and the Block cottages associated with Staveley's Speedwell Colliery. The Speedwell once occupied part of the Ireland colliery site and was one of the mid-19th century shallow coal mines superseded by a new generation of deep-level pits in the latter part of the century. These miners' cottages were good quality industrial housing for their time but obviously already derelict by May 15th, 1965 when Staveley's O4/6 no. 63913, with a Caution for Staveley South Junction, eased gently by heading for the foot of the bank with a class K local coal train, almost certainly from Arkwright Colliery.

Syd Hancock

….. and on no. 63913 goes, towards Staveley South Junction. The Chesterfield loop can be seen converging from the left, whilst to the right another O4 'Tiny' heads tender first along the Markham branch, alongside Staveley shed's coaling stage. No. 63913 has much in common with no. 63914 whom we just met on the Markham colliery line. She too originated as a 5'6" boilered class 8M, Great Central Railway no. 11 built at Gorton in August, 1919. In her case rebuilding from LNER class O5 to O4 took place in May 1936, and this is how no. 63914 also would have looked prior to her further rebuild with a 100A boiler. The O4/6 sub-classification signified that she has a wider cab than a standard O4, that and her vertical slot cab front lookouts is a legacy of having to fit around her original large boiler. Owing her successive owners nothing, no. 63913 lasted until June, 1965.   *Syd Hancock*

From the same viewpoint, a footbridge which once gave the Speedwell estate's miners a short-cut to Ireland Colliery, LMS 'Jubilee' no. 45581 *Bihar and Orissa* (North British Loco., October, 1934) climbs away from the South Junction with the June 27th, 1964 Bradford – Poole. Thanks to Syd Hancock we shall be seeing the Saturdays only Bradford – Poole and its return working several times on our way to Nottingham. A Great Central institution until the Midland Region, in its systematic and cynical starvation of the GC main line, transferred it to the Midland line in the summer of 1965, the train was invariably worked by a Farnley Junction 'Jubilee', *Bihar and Orissa* being one of the regular performers. She would remain at Farnley Junction until withdrawal in August 1966. The Markham Colliery lines are choc-a-bloc with wagons but those on the left are from Staveley Works, for which a connection had been retained when the Chesterfield loop closed, over a year before.   *Syd Hancock*

Turning the clock back we have a fine panorama at Staveley South Junction, as the Great Central Railway's splendid war memorial locomotive *Valour* – and it can be no other with that depth of nameplate – storms up the bank. In the left distance the Chesterfield loop swings away to the west, while to the right are the Markham Colliery branch and Staveley shed's coaling stage. *Valour* emerged from Gorton in July 1920 as Great Central Class 9P no. 1165. Never rebuilt, she was withdrawn as class B3 no. 1496 on the very last day of the LNER's existence, December 31st, 1947. ***G. Perrin collection***

STAVELEY SHED

Before continuing south we have time for a last look round Staveley shed, beginning with a reminder of how it looked in its halcyon days, with twelve roads beneath a pristine northlight roof. The locomotive complement includes a couple of 8A/Q4 0-8-0s, mineral engine predecessors of the iconic 8K/O4, which also usurped their 'Tinies' nickname – whereupon the 0-8-0s became 'Proper Tinies' ! There is also a 9J/J11 'Pom-Pom', partly hidden behind the chassis of a double-framed 0-6-0 with curved frames – just possibly a Sacré 6A 'Bulldog' but more than likely a Parker 6AI/J8 'Basher', all twelve of which ended their days at Staveley between 1926 and 1930. ***W. Wagstaffe***

Former Great Central class 8A no. 92, as the LNER's Q4 no. 5092, looking very smart (despite having had that abomination of a chimney inflicted upon her by the LNER) posing in front of the original Staveley shed in 1931. No. 5092 (Kitson, November 1903) was a Staveley engine from February, 1924 until August, 1943. She was renumbered 3212 under the LNER 1946 scheme but, although surviving into the British Railways era, she was withdrawn from Barnsley in May, 1949 without ever carrying her allocated BR no. 63212.

Gordon Coltas

By 1951 Staveley shed's northlight roof had deteriorated badly and BR rebuilt the shed, but the new transverse pitched roofing only covered five roads as can be seen behind O4/3 no. 63735. Only the west side range of offices and workshops, glimpsed above the WD, retained their northlight roof profile. On the eastern side the other seven roads still remained, now in the open, but were increasingly utilised for the storage of out of service locomotives. The absence of a vacuum brake pipe on her buffer beam identifies no 63735, standing back to back with an unidentified O1, as an ex-ROD, no. 1805 built by North British Loco's Queen's Park Works and shipped straight over to France in September, 1917. After repatriation and a spell on loan to the Great Central Railway, she mouldered in the Morecambe dump from August, 1921 until being one of that last batch bought for a song by the LNER in February, 1927. Unsurprisingly she wasn't able to enter traffic before that October but then, as is apparent from her photograph, she remained unaltered until, as old soldiers do, she faded away in December, 1962.

D.F. Barton

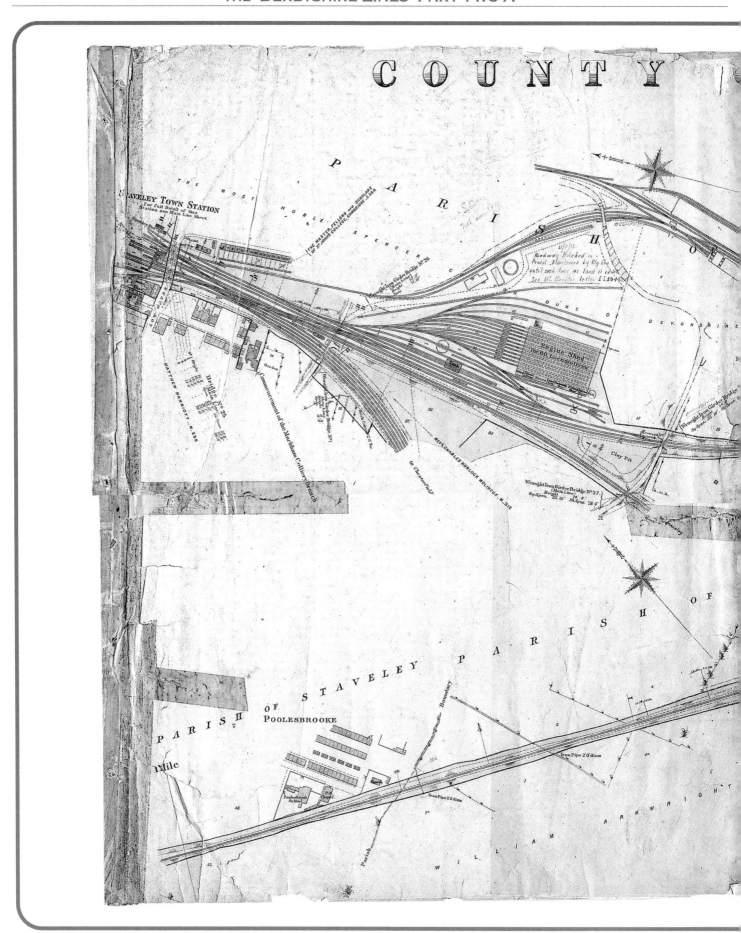

Standing back, the foundations of the original 12 road shed are clearly visible, though by this date (1959 ?) the outermost two roads have been lifted. In the distance, the MS&L built Railway Cottages (post-railway re-Christened Belmont Drive) rise up to the Worksop road, upon which stands Staveley Central station's booking office. The forlorn looking row of locomotives on the right have the tell-tale 'stored out of service' sacking over their chimneys. Beyond a couple of 0-6-2 tanks are three D11 'Directors', the nearest one 62667, *Somme* (Gorton, November 1922). Latterly, the 'Directors' were all stored for the winter months, then brought back for the summer services, so she will still have another summer left in her. Apart from *Mons*, withdrawn in May, 1959, all disappeared during 1960, *Somme* that August. Within the old shed area, the nearer row of locomotives again have their chimneys covered, with more 'Directors' behind an ex-ROD O4/3 no. 63771. She was built for the ROD as no. 1864 by North British Loco's Hyde Park Works in April, 1918 and, after spells in France and on loan to the Great Western bought by the LNER in March, 1924. She too will have quite a bit more work to do before her withdrawal in November, 1962. The lines of locomotives still in service are dominated by 2-8-0s, unsurprisingly at this overwhelmingly freight shed in the heart of the Derbyshire and North Nottinghamshire coalfield. Next to 63771 is another O4/3, which looks to be no. 63665 (Kitsons ROD no. 1627 of September 1918, withdrawn December, 1963). Alongside her, someone has been considerate enough to clean the smokebox number plate of no. 63749. She also started out as a ROD, North British Loco's Queens Park Works no. 1829 of November, 1917, sent to France in January, 1918. After being repatriated she was one of 26 briefly loaned to the Lancashire and Yorkshire Railway (where they were found to be a rather tight fit !) then to the LNWR, their no. 2965, from June, 1920 until recalled to become one of nearly 200 in the Queensferry dump, in August, 1921. She rusted there until finally purchased at a knock down price by the LNER in February, 1927, though its hardly surprising that it then took them until April, 1928 to have her fit for traffic. She saw out her career as an O4/7, as seen here, after her May, 1940 rebuild with a shortened O2-type boiler, in October, 1959, thus giving us a latest possible date for this quite fascinating photograph.

Neville Stead collection

There's still though plenty of life in this pair of O4s, nos. 63604 and 63611, standing beside the new eastern wall on what would have been covered roads prior to the shed's rebuilding. Both were original Great Central class 8K 'Tinies' (LNER class O4/1), Gorton built, no. 63604 as GC no. 379 in June, 1913, no. 63611 as GC no. 386 in January, 1914. No. 63611 remained in her original condition to the end, which for her came in March, 1964, but 63604 was rebuilt as an O4/8 with a 100A boiler in January, 1954. It made little difference: she went in May, 1964.

Peter Groom

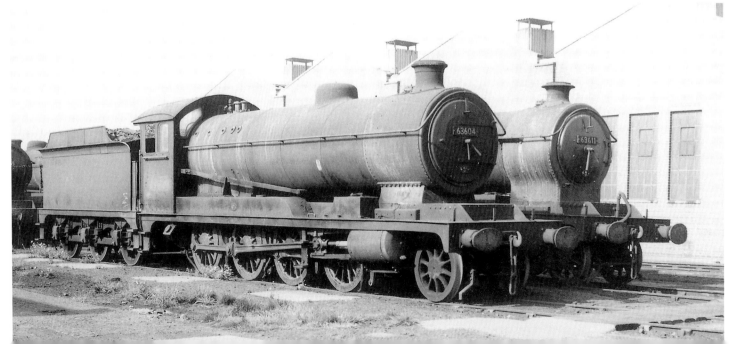

More 2-8-0s, with another ex-ROD O4/3 no. 63685 obviously stored. As well as the ROD's characteristic absence of the original Great Central engines' vacuum brake pipe, at this proximity the buffer beam sockets are apparent, into which continental-style side chains would have been fitted when she was delivered by Robert Stephenson & Co. as ROD no. 1667 in January, 1918. Her history was not untypical: after returning from France she was on loan to the L&NWR (their no. 2912) from December, 1919 until August, 1921, then one of the LNER's earlier purchases from the Queensferry dump in December, 1923. A real bargain, she lasted until March, 1964. Over by the wall, representing the ROD's World War 2 counterpart, is WD class 2-8-0 no. 90030, looking very spruce for a 'Dub-Dee'. Built by North British Loco. in 1943 as WD no. 77254, she was one of the 200 purchased by the LNER (class O7) and numbered 3030. Whether she might briefly have carried the number 63030 before the whole class was renumbered in the 90XXX series is not known. For a short-term wartime expedient she didn't do at all badly, finally being withdrawn from Goole shed in April, 1967. Between the two old soldiers is a genuine class 8K, O4/1 no. 63690, the Great Central Railway's no. 1188, built by Kitson in July, 1912. She lasted until December, 1962. *C.Machin*

Around at the western side of the shed where the northlight profile was retained, the immediate impression is how very much superior was the original brickwork. It forms the backdrop to another old soldier, ex-ROD no. 63847, looking quite presentable in the earlier 'fifties at her home shed. She had been ROD no. 2046, by North British Loco's Hyde Park Works in May, 1919, as construction was continued after the end of the Great War to obviate unemployment. She was loaned to the L&NW, their no. 2837, until August, 1921, then purchased by the LNER from the Queensferry dump in December, 1923. Thus far its a familiar story, but then she was one of 10 modified by the LNER with lower chimneys and even flat strapping in place of the usual 'L' section cab-roof bracing, to fit within the former North British Railway's restricted loading gauge for service in the Fifeshire coalfield. Six more followed later and all were classified O4/2. As seen, she ended her days south of the border but became surplus to requirements here too in May, 1959.

In what even by Staveley standards is a truly pitiable state, B1 no. 61155 ruminates on the wrongs done to steam engines. She should be in her prime, only having been delivered from Vulcan Foundry in May, 1947. She will be gone by March, 1964 but, goodness, that was longer than many others managed !

If there was one locomotive type in which the Great Central was deficient, it was the short wheelbase, go anywhere shunting tank, just what was needed to negotiate the threepenny-bit curves so often to be found in colliery and works yards. The Great Eastern had legions of them, at one time mainstays of the Liverpool Street 'Jazz' suburbans for which their rapid acceleration was ideal, but their short wheelbase was a major factor in the jerky riding which earned them their nickname of 'Buckjumpers' – more ruefully affectionate than critical, one suspects. What perky little engines they looked, with their front boiler-ring mounted domes. Some later judicious relocation of the Great Eastern tanks made good the Great Central's shortage. Which is how Staveley came by James Holden's J69 no. 68591 (the Great Eastern's class R24 no. 203, December 1899), lately arrived from her Stratford birthplace to see out her time until January, 1960. She will find knocking a few wagons around such as Ireland Colliery yard a far cry from dashing between Bethnal Green and Cambridge Heath.

Howard Turner

With Staveley's coaling stage in the background, this is the Great Central's idea of a shunting tank, or rather the Manchester, Sheffield and Lincolnshire's, for N5 no. 69309 was built by Beyer Peacock as Great Central class 9F no. 769 in July, 1898 to Thomas Parker's MS&L design of 1893. The N5s were equally adept on a stopping passenger, or a pick-up goods, but their longer wheelbase was ill-suited to the tight corners 68591 could manage. No. 69309 arrived at Staveley in November, 1955 and will see out her time here in November, 1960. That chimney is not the Great Central's fault.

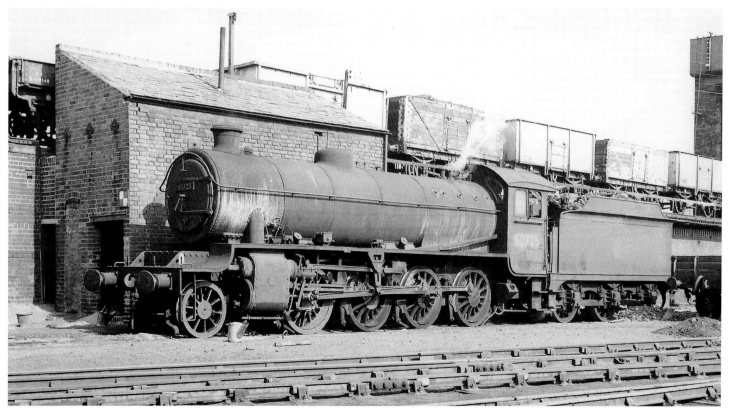

O1 no. 63725 basking in the sunshine, beside the sandhouse and the ramp up to the coaling stage in May, 1964. She had been a stalwart of the Annesley – Woodford 'Runners' between 1950 and 1956, before finally settling at Staveley in November, 1963. Originally a ROD, no. 1641 (Robert Stephenson's, August 1919), she was too late to see service in France and went straight on loan to the LNWR (their no. 2832). After being recalled to Queensferry she was snapped up by the LNER in December, 1923 and, like no. 63847 whom we just met, trimmed down for service as an O4/2 in the Fifeshire coalfield. Rebuilt to her final O1 form in March, 1945 she will bow out in July, 1965.

Peter Groom

With a gaggle of 'spotters' aboard, D11 no. 62663 *Prince Albert* (GC class 11F no. 509, Gorton, March 1920) has just topped-up at Staveley's coaling stage, beside the turntable. An odd one out amongst the 2-8-0s which served Staveley's almost wholly freight duties, when the rest of the 'Directors' came home to Darnall in 1958 for their all too brief swansong after wanderings about Lincolnshire and the Cheshire Lines, *Prince Albert* was given charge of Staveley's one and only passenger turn. It included the 'Spitfire', the 5.49 pm Sheffield Victoria – Leicester Central all stations, which had earned its nickname from the snappy turn round required at Leicester, where only 23 minutes were allowed for shunting the train, turning the locomotive and having her ready for the return. Apart from 62665 *Mons*, which had gone in May, 1959, the class was still intact into 1960, but then *Prince Albert* went that May. By the end of the year they were all gone, the last one no. 62666 *Zeebrugge*.

Neville Stead collection

Staveley was never favoured with a 'cenotaph' coaling tower, managing to the end with the labour-intensive coaling stage beneath its water tank. Wagons of locomotive coal were propelled up the ramp, then emptied into small tubs which were pushed along the 'drawbridges' seen here, and tipped bodily into the tender of the locomotive waiting below. Very hard, filthy work but at least it didn't reduce the coal to dust.

M.A.King

Just south of Staveley, where the Duckmanton road dog legs under the line, O4/8 no. 63706 comes down the bank in 1964 with a short mineral train, probably from Arkwright Colliery. At least this lightweight load holds no threat of overcoming the engine and guard's brake power – an ever present danger on downhill gradients in those loose coupled wagon days. No. 63706 is yet another ex-ROD 'old soldier' – what a bargain they were for the LNER. Built by Robert Stephenson & Co. as ROD no. 1650 in October, 1918, she was just in time to see some service in France before being loaned to the Great Western as their no. 3049 from November, 1919 until recalled to the Beachley dump in January, 1922. She was purchased by the LNER in December, 1923 and would initially have gone into traffic as an O4/3, but in May, 1940 was rebuilt with a shortened O2-type boiler as an O4/7. She was again rebuilt as the O4/8 seen here, with a 100A boiler in November, 1956 which saw her career through to September, 1965. What stories she could have told. *Bob Tebb*

Stanier 8F 2-8-0s were never commonplace on the Great Central, though Annesley had a few in the early 'sixties where they earned a grudging respect – for a "Midland" engine ! No. 48293 was an Annesley engine between September 1962 and July, 1965 and has something in common with so many of the O4s we've met, she's another old soldier, built for the War Department by Beyer Peacock in 1940 but taken into LMS stock in 1943. She looks to be going well up the bank, near Inkersall. She will be withdrawn from Lostock Hall in June, 1968. *Cliff Machin*

Just a little further up the bank we again meet WD no. 90030, whom we last encountered on shed at Staveley, just about to cross over the turnouts of Duckmanton North Junction with another class H goods. Duckmanton South's distant is 'on' but at the speed she will be going, the only worry about that is the thought of perhaps being brought to a halt and then having to restart on the gradient. She's about three miles up the 1-in-100 bank from Staveley, with about as much still to go before the climb eases beyond Heath. You can just imagine her, shouldering along with that characteristic WD gait, her exhaust vying with the rhythmic bump-clank-bump-clank as loose-fitting coupling rods lift and drop. The enginemen will be standing on the coal continually shaken down by her endemic dreadful riding. Unlovely and unloved as they then were, we can now look back upon them with nostalgic affection.   *Cliff Machin*

From about the same place (a handy occupation bridge on the footpath from Calow to the long-defunct "Ducky Works") but on the opposite side of the track, O1 no. 63630 has a clear road with up iron ore empties, round about 1960. No. 63630 has trodden a by now familiar path: ROD no. 1712 (Nasmith Wilson, February, 1918) one of 50 loaned to the Caledonian – where they were nicknamed 'Froggies' and thoroughly disliked (the Caley was a left-hand drive line) – rescued by the LNER from Gretna but not until February, 1927, so they did well to have her de-rusted and in traffic by that May. She was rebuilt to an O1 in June, 1945, which means of course that of the original O4 more or less only the chassis and tender remained. She was one of 53 out of the total number of 58 O1s which pretty well monopolised Annesley's Woodford 'Runners' until they were displaced by the 9F 'Spaceships', when she became a Staveley engine to the end, which for her came in July, 1965.

David Grainger

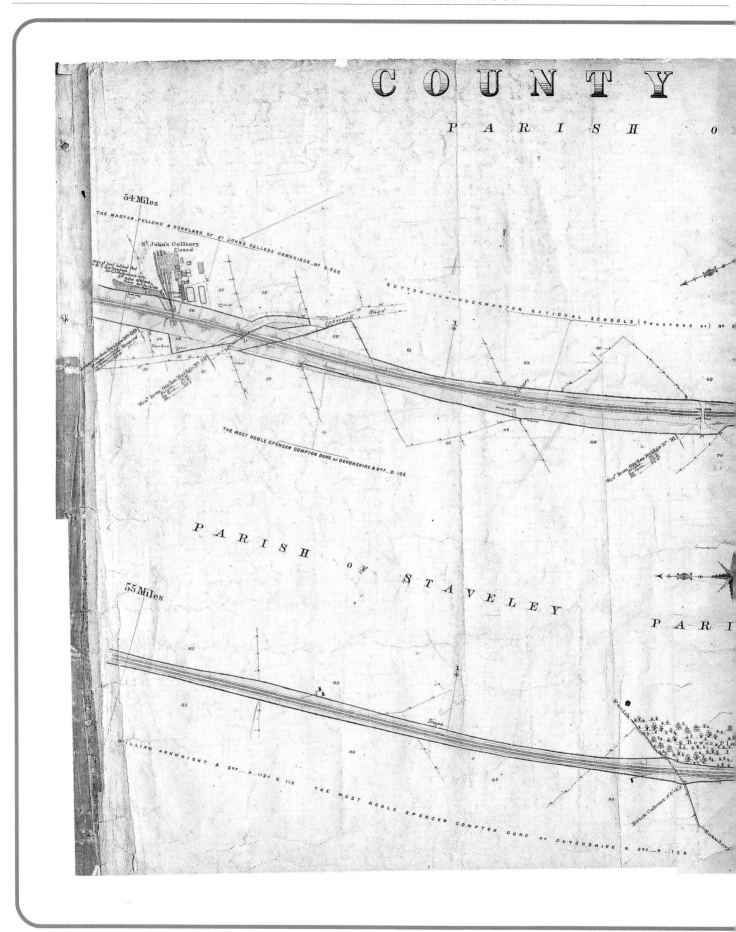

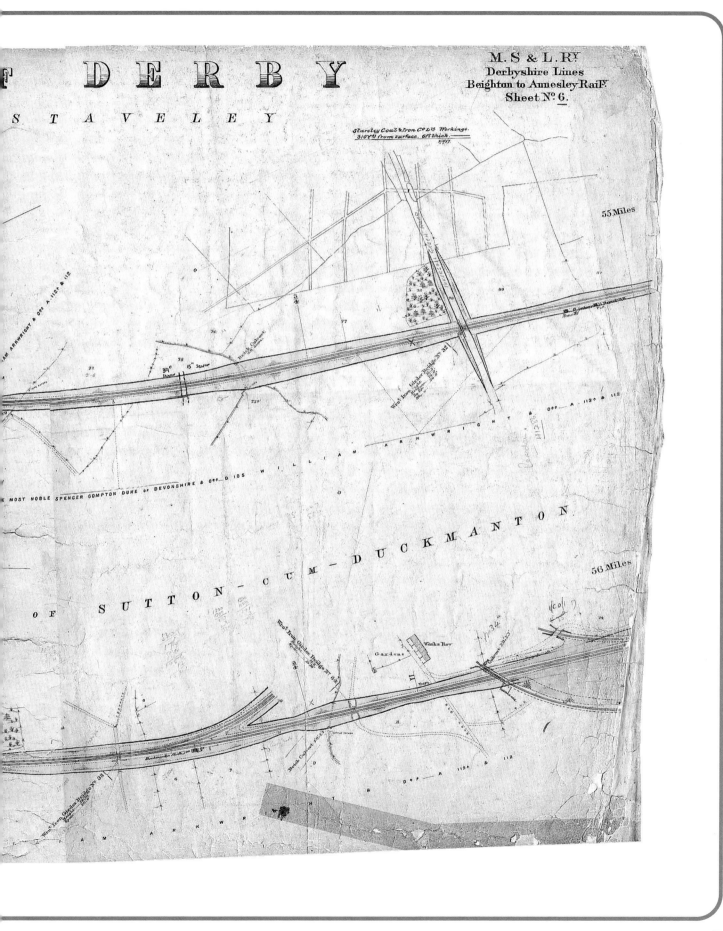

Looking south from that same occupation bridge in the mid-fifties, an unidentified V2 is tearing past Duckmanton North Junction 'box and headlong down the bank with a through express from the south coast, composed of carriages tantalisingly in Southern green. In those days, the south coast seemed a very, very long way away, and trains manifestly having come from that remote land added immeasurably to the Great Central's allure. We are within a mile of Sutton Springwood tunnel, which is fully on the 1-in-100 downgrade but had pretty tight clearances for a V2 or an A3. Therefore, to avoid risking a blowback, they came through the tunnel with power on. Result: at Duckmanton Junction they were flying ! The Duckmanton junctions originated from the Great Central's 1906 gazumping of the Great Northern's attempted takeover of the Lancashire, Derbyshire and East Coast Railway. Kings Cross had tried to drive too hard a bargain, which allowed the Great Central to step in with a better offer and, in truth, scotch what would have been a Great Northern arrow pointing straight at its Sheffield heart. The LD&EC became part of the Great Central with effect from January 1st, 1907, but in addition to having effected a junction with the LD&EC's Beighton branch at Killamarsh, the Great Central had placed a contract to connect the two lines at Duckmanton, where they crossed at right angles, fully six months earlier. Despite needing some heavy earthworks and not insignificant bridges, the junctions were fully operational by the end of September, 1907.   ***David Grainger***

Demonstrating Duckmanton North Junction's prime purpose, Staveley's O4/3 no. 63701 is just coming onto the main line with coal from Arkwright Colliery. From here its an easy run down the bank for her crew, their only concern will be to keep their unbraked train in check. This was also the route taken by the Staveley – Chesterfield Market Place goods, which operated from the 1951 isolation of the former LD&EC's Market Place terminus by the line's severance at Bolsover, until the western extremity was abandoned in 1957. Duckmanton North Junction 'box is again visible above the locomotive's tender, while the bridge above the rear of the train carries the down line connection of Duckmanton South's flying junction. No. 63701's story is becoming a familiar one: ROD no. 1684, built by Robert Stephenson in July, 1918, but was then one of the batch loaned after the War to the Great Eastern Railway, before being recalled to the Aintree dump from where she was purchased by the LNER in February, 1925. She will soldier on until August, 1965, by when she will have outlived Staveley shed and, indeed, Great Central line through freights altogether.   ***Cliff Machin***

Another consignment of Arkwright colliery coal heads for Duckmanton North Junction, on March 31st, 1964, behind Staveley's O4/8 no. 63612, though her class H 'Through Goods' headcode perhaps implies her destination might be somewhere further afield than Staveley. In this rarely photographed location, looking south from the Chesterfield – Bolsover road, to the east of Arkwright Town, no. 63612 has just passed Arkwright Town Junction signal box, in the 'V' of its junction with the former LD&EC line, and is about to pass the bracket signal which formerly guarded Duckmanton East Junction, though the absence of an arm for Duckmanton South Junction's up connection indicates that has already gone. But just look at the track and ballast on what is, after all, only a colliery connection. Immaculate ! No. 63612 was an original Great Central 8K, No. 387 built at Gorton in January 1914. She was rebuilt as an O4/8 as late as July, 1955. She will remain at Staveley until its closure in June 1965, but will then only survive at Langwith Junction until that November.

Syd Hancock

Duckmanton East Junction 'box on May 18th,1964, a month before it was finally demolished. Its lever fame has already been dismantled along with, as is apparent, the connections to the South Junction leaving the, by now, just single line connection to the North Junction. The box looks remarkably pristine. Had it been repainted shortly before closure ? 'Twas ever the kiss of death !

Syd Hancock

Looking in the opposite direction, the connection from Arkwright Town Junction on the former LD&EC can be seen arcing away to join the Great Central line by Duckmanton North Junction signal box, visible immediately to the right of the East Junction box. Just discernible on the extreme right of the photograph is the occupation bridge from which the earlier photographs of Duckmanton North Junction were taken. Happy days.   *Syd Hancock*

There had certainly been no late repainting of Arkwright Town Junction signal box, awaiting its fate on July 12th, 1964, in fact it looks dubious whether it had ever been repainted since it was first commissioned in 1907 ! The view is eastwards, towards Lincoln, along what had been the LD&EC main line until mining subsidence damage to Bolsover tunnel and Carr Vale viaduct enforced the line's severance at Langwith Junction in 1951. The effects of subsidence are readily apparent here, where a ground frame now suffices to control the singled line connection to Duckmanton North Junction passing behind the box. Beyond are the beginnings of the opencast mining which will, ultimately, obliterate all signs of the railway here.   *Syd Hancock*

As luck would have it, just as Duckmanton North Junction is overlooked by a convenient occupation bridge, there is a fine view of Duckmanton South Junction from another Chesterfield – Bolsover road bridge, about half a mile west of that from which we were looking at Arkwright Town Junction. In contrast with the North Junction, the Great Central provided a flying junction at Duckmanton South, with the down connection to the former Lancashire, Derbyshire and East Coast veering away to the west before swinging back over the girder bridge in the distance, thus avoiding any disruption of up line traffic. It and the up connection join the lines from the North Junction at Duckmanton East Junction, from where they arc southwards to the Arkwright Town Junction with the ex-LD&EC Chesterfield to Lincoln line, which crosses under the Great Central just behind our vantage point. The importance of all this elaboration was fish. The reason for the Grimsby fish traffic to the Great Central cannot be overstated: as well as fish vans frequently being added to the rear of passenger trains, complete trains hurried to the south and to the west country at express passenger speeds. The Great Central's takeover of the LD&EC offered a short cut for the traffic, with trains taking the Market Rasen line to reach the former LD&EC at Lincoln, then gaining the main line here at Duckmanton. Within ten years though, in September 1916, the Mansfield Railway opened, giving a connection from Clipstone on the LD&EC via

Mansfield Central to Kirkby South Junction, an even shorter route which made Duckmanton South Junction largely redundant. Duckmanton South Junction – Fish – it is totally appropriate to illustrate the junction with the New Clee – Banbury 'Whitland Fish' storming through on May 27th, 1954, but, in view of the foregoing, it is ironic that this train took the original route, heading west along the old MS&L line then taking the Waleswood Curve to reach the main line at Killamarsh Junction, south-east of Sheffield. This train was something of a star turn, almost invariably headed by a pair of K3 'Jazzers' - double-headers were a rarity on the Great Central, so what a disappointment to find that the double-heading was merely an operational convenience. The 'Whitland Fish' was an Immingham working and the train engine, no. 61836 (originally LNER no. 125, Darlington, January 1925) is indeed an Immingham engine. Her pilot though, no. 61975 (originally LNER no. 3815, Darlington, November, 1936) is an Annesley engine, just working back home. She might come off at Annesley South Junction but will more probably trundle back light to her home shed after the train stops for inspection at Nottingham Victoria. No. 61975 will be withdrawn from Bradford Low Moor in September, 1961, outlasting no. 61836, withdrawn from Doncaster in February, 1960.

Ken Boulter

We've stepped back northwards just a few yards as York shed's B1 no. 61002 *Impala* hurries by, deputising for the usual B16 'Bloodspitter' with a York – Banbury fitted goods. Duckmanton North Junction box and the adjacent occupation bridge are just visible under Duckmanton South Junction's down line girder bridge flyover. Only the third B1 built (originally LNER no. 8303, Darlington, September 1943), *Impala* will have had a longer service life than any of her sisters when she is finally withdrawn in June, 1967. *Cliff Machin*

Further north still, on November 28th, 1964 we're looking south from what was Duckmanton South Junction's down line flyover, by now lifted. Staveley shed's O4/3 no. 63701, whom we have already met at Duckmanton North Junction, has just come under the road bridge from which we were admiring the 'Whitland Fish', heading for home with coal empties. On the skyline to the left of the road bridge is Arkwright Town's old school, while further to the left are the roofs and chimneys of Arkwright Town's terraces. When they were found to be acting as gas collectors for methane percolating up from Arkwright Colliery's old coal workings, Arkwright Town (actually never more than a village) was transplanted, lock, stock and barrel, a few hundred yards across the Chesterfield – Bolsover road, a move completed by 1995. So from this photograph, not only no. 63701 and the Great Central main line but even the village has gone ! *A. Smalley*

Left: We're back at the turnouts of Duckmanton South Junction as Woodford Halse's V2 no. 60831 thunders by with a mid-fifties up 'Master Cutler'. Until it was transferred to the Kings Cross line in the wake of "London Midlandisation" in 1958, the 'Cutler' was the showpiece of the Great Central line, but only infrequently photographed towards its Sheffield end – the 7.40 or 7.50 am departure time was a bit early, and its 10 pm return far too late for most cameramen! No. 60831 was originally the LNER's no. 4802, built at Darlington in May, 1938. Her outside steam pipes indicate she has been latterly rebuilt with three separate cylinders in place of the original 'monobloc' casting – but whatever the practicalities, the rebuilds just didn't have the same sleekness, did they? She will be one of the last two V2s in service when she is withdrawn from York (North) shed in December, 1966.

Graham Perrin collection

Below: Could there be any greater contrast between yesterday's railways and those of today ? Even if there was still a railway here, unchecked verdure would ensure that there could be no present-day counterpart of this view of O1 no. 63863, passing Duckmanton South Junction with an up coal train. As it is, Duckmanton South Junction's layout is portrayed in full, the down connection swinging away to cross over the main line, with catch points protecting the main line from any runaways, while the up connection runs parallel with the main line until it climbs away to the East Junction just beyond the rear of the train. No. 63863 was originally North British Loco's Hyde Park Works ROD no. 2074 of August, 1919. Too late for service in France, she was one of those loaned to the North Eastern, where they were less than popular with the enginemen who, contrasting their arc-sided cabs with Worsdell and Raven engines' commodious side-window cabs, nicknamed them "pneumonia engines" ! Presumably she wouldn't have been too much missed when she was recalled to Aintree in 1921, to be picked up by the LNER in February, 1925. She was rebuilt to class O1 in September, 1945 (including the side window cab, which might have made her more appreciated in the North East). In this Autumn, 1963 view she had only recently arrived at Staveley, that June, and will remain there until the shed closes in June, 1965.

Syd Hancock

On May 3rd, 1951, against a panoramic backdrop of Duckmanton South Junction, Annesley's O4/2 no. 63674 is about to pass under the Arkwright road bridge. On the right hand side, the 'home' signal guarding the up connection from the LD&EC has a sighting board, to aid visibility against the dark background of the road bridge. The gradient post on the left indicates that no. 63674 has breasted a mini-summit, but its only a momentary easing on the 1-in-100 ascent. No. 63674 will leave Annesley in October, 1952, but she won't go far, alternating between Staveley and Colwick for the rest of her career. She's already had plenty of adventures, and has more to come: originally Robert Stephenson's ROD no. 1655 of October, 1917, after service in France she first went on loan to the Lancashire and Yorkshire then, when the RODs proved to be too tight a fit for the L&Y, to the London and North Western (their no. 2958) from June 1920 until she was recalled to the Queensferry dump in August, 1921. Rescued from there in December, 1923, like no. 63847 whom we met at Staveley shed, she was amongst those selected for adaptation to the former North British Railway's restricted loading gauge, for service in the Fifeshire coalfield before returning south. Not finished yet, she will see out her time until January, 1966 as an O4/8, after being rebuilt in May, 1957. **Ken Boulter**

A summer, 1963 view southwards from the Arkwright Town road bridge, as Woodford Halse's Stanier class 5 no. 45116 (Vulcan Foundry, June 1935) hurries down the bank past Duckmanton South Junction signal box, with a train of Southern green empty coaching stock. The subsidiary signals control the South Junction's down connection to the former LD&EC, but no. 45116 has a clear road along the down main. No. 45116 will have left the GC, never to return, by the end of the year, and will end her days at Wigan Springs Branch, in July 1967. **Syd Hancock**

Why Duckmanton South Junction signal box was sited so far away from the junction, on the other side of the Arkwright road bridge, is not apparent. The bridge impeded the signalman's view and he would most certainly have had some long lever pulls. Like that at the North Junction, the signal box is of a later pattern, with its entry porch akin to those of the 'London Extension' Type 4 we shall see south of Annesley, but its 1907 installation actually postdated the evolution of the Great Central's final, Type 5 'box.

Just a few hundred yards beyond Duckmanton South Junction and the crossing over the LD&EC line to Chesterfield, still climbing at 1-in-100 the Derbyshire Lines threaded Sutton Spring Wood tunnel. It wasn't really a tunnel at all and there would have needed to be no more than quite a shallow cutting had not the local landowner, William Arkwright of Sutton Scarsdale Hall, insisted upon the cut-and-cover passage through Sutton Spring Wood. Obviously William Arkwright was not anti-railway as were some landowners who insisted on railways being kept out of their sight, he was actively projecting his Lancashire, Derbyshire and East Coast Railway even as the MS&L Derbyshire Lines were being built, but he was a keen huntsman and didn't want the railway to spoil his sport. As remarked earlier, clearances through Sutton Spring Wood tunnel, were a bit tight for larger engines, though whether this had always been so or was the result of pitfalls is not clear – perhaps significantly the MS&L's 2-chain plans indicate the depths of coal seams beneath the tunnel: the 'Deep Hards' seam 150 yards below; the 'Tupton' seam 210 yards down; then the 'Black Shale' at 270 yards. Whether or not coal workings had affected the original clearances, stated to be 22 ft high and 26 ft span, despite being on the 1-in-100 downgrade, A3 or V2 headed down trains shot through with power on. There were no such considerations with up trains which were working hard anyway, and on Saturday, May 18th, 1963 the line has exalted company with the preserved LNER A3 no. 4472 *Flying Scotsman* erupting out of the tunnel's south portal and on up the bank with the Gainsborough Model Railway Society's Lincoln to Southampton Central 'GMRS Isle of Wight Special'. *Flying Scotsman* should feel quite at home: a decade earlier, as Leicester Central's (usually rather scruffy) no. 60103, this had been her stamping ground with regular visits to Sheffield Victoria. ***Cliff Machin***

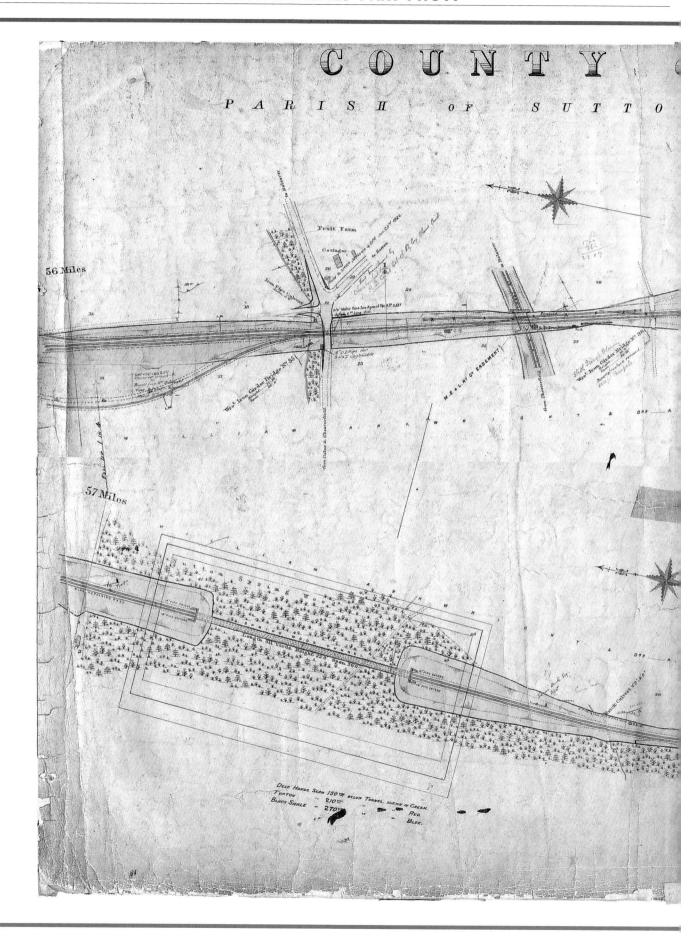

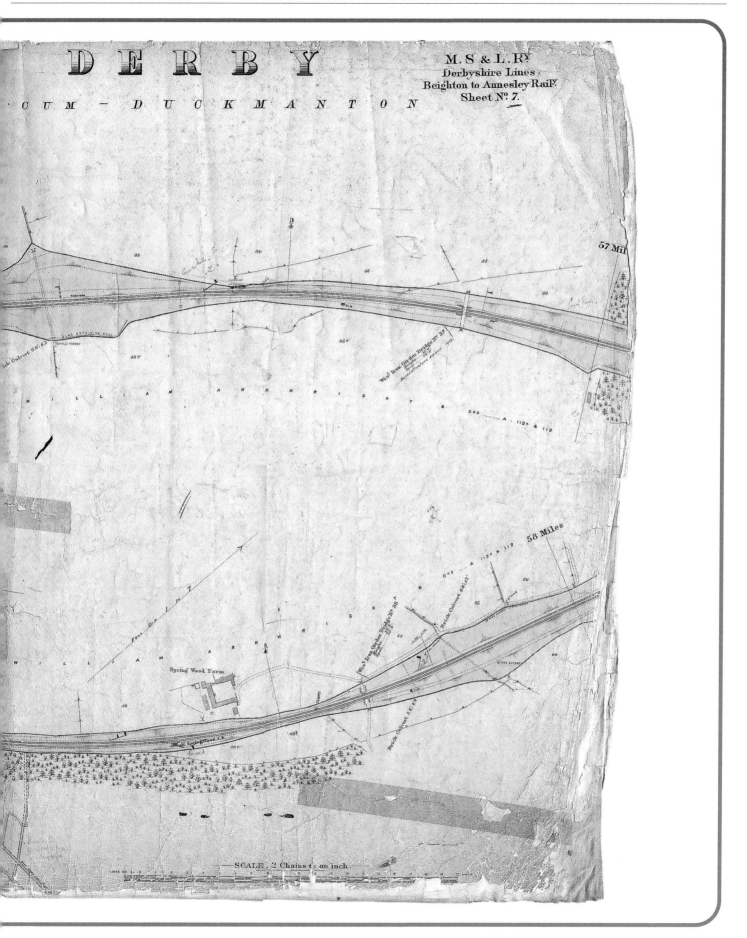

From the same foot crossing a more typical working and no doubt at a more typical speed emerges from Sutton Spring Wood Tunnel's south portal: a Class 'H' through goods behind Stanier 8F no. 48064 (Vulcan Foundry, November 1936). The stipulation that the line should be in tunnel obviously didn't specify the quality of the infill, which was a sterile grey slag, even sixty years on defying all but the sparsest scrub to get a toehold and presenting no impediment to two boys (the author and his brother) watching a slow moving goods enter the tunnel's north end, then dashing its 311 yard length to see the train slogging on its way from the south end. And then there are the memories of being lulled to sleep on a frosty night, some miles away in the village of Calow, by the resonating measured beat as one mineral train after another blasted its way up from Staveley. Happy, happy days. No. 48064 was an Annesley engine from September, 1962 until she returned to home territory at Derby in May, 1964. Withdrawal came in May, 1966. *Cliff Machin*

A more typical eruption from Sutton Spring Wood tunnel on March 23rd, 1963, heralds the emergence of what is beginning to be a familiar companion, WD no. 90030, with yet another class H goods but, for once, not the usual mineral wagons. The state of the track and ballast is what would be expected on this award winning prize length. Immaculate. *R. Blencowe collection*

HEATH

And so back to Heath, where an earlier 1950s up express has just passed Heath Junction 'box, seen above the rear of the train, and is about to power through Heath station. Putting up a magnificent exhaust – and doing her best to hide Heath's goods yard – the engine is an original 'monobloc' cylindered V2, in all likelihood a Leicester engine, but her grubbiness tantalisingly doesn't allow her number to be made out.   ***Bill Hudson***

Also about to pass through Heath station but at a rather steadier pace, 'Dub-Dee' no. 90285 has just brought another up coal train past Heath Junction 'box in the left distance. She still has some work to do to reach the summit at Pilsley but, with the gradient now easing, the worst is over. The Williamthorpe colliery branch, descending to cross under the Chesterfield loop junction, is again prominent on the right but by now, May 14th, 1965, Heath's goods shed and yard have been transformed into the wasteland on the left. No. 90285 was a December, 1943 product of North British Loco., WD no. 77411. Formerly an Immingham engine, she had come to Retford (Thrumpton) in September, 1963 but is now very much in her final days. She will be withdrawn the following month, June 1965.   ***J.S.Hancock***

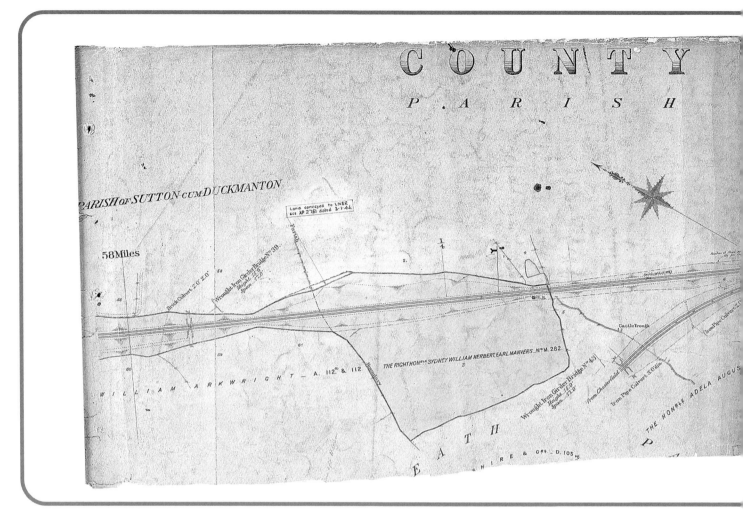

Retracing our steps northwards, beyond the site of Heath Junction, we again meet Farnley Junction 'Jubilee' no. 45581 *Bihar and Orissa* with the Bradford – Poole. At this point, immediately after bridging the 'Chesterfield – Mansfield road and the connection into Williamthorpe Colliery, the Chesterfield loop lines are converging from the left, but by this date, August 22nd, 1964, they are out of use, weed covered and ready for lifting. *J.S.Hancock*

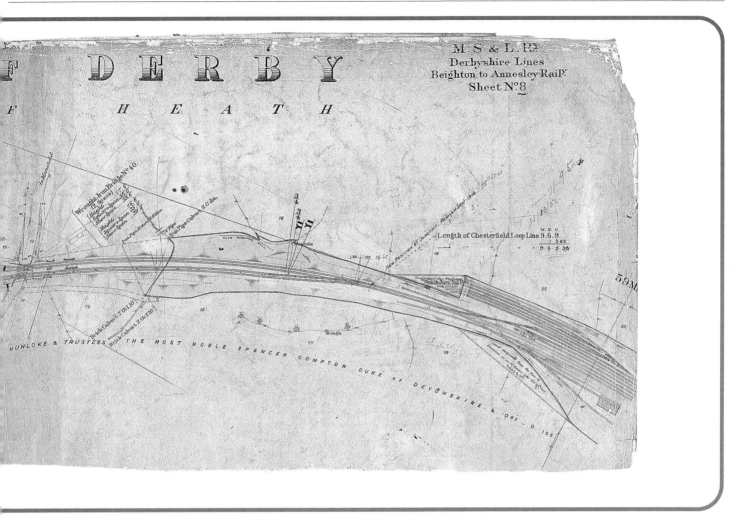

Darnall's B1 no. 61152 (Vulcan Foundry, May 1947) is bringing an up local into the station on May 12th, 1956, beneath the Heath Road bridge from which the Heath Junction photographs were taken. The road connects the mining community of Holmewood, which grew up alongside the station, with Heath village, a little way to the east. The down line signals will be noted, sited on the up side for clear visibility through the station curve, with splitting distants for either the main line or, on the left, the Chesterfield loop. No. 61152 will outlive Heath station by just over a year, until April, 1964. **Henry Priestley**

A few local lads have congregated to be in the picture in this early view of Heath station, as it first opened to passengers on January 2nd, 1893, prior to the destruction and replacement of the main, down side buildings. A sawtooth facade has been applied to the station building, to accept the standard ridge and furrow platform canopy, and as usual on Derbyshire Lines stations the subsidiary platform building was built to that same profile. Whether the canopies were actually built has yet to be established, but if not then Heath would have been the only Derbyshire Lines station not provided with them.

Below Left: It was at Heath that the author's old friend and mentor Herbert Ashton, latterly station foreman at Chesterfield Central where we met him in 'Derbyshire Lines Part 1', commenced his employment with the Great Central Railway, as this 16 year-old lad porter, in 1918. He had already worked for two years at the local colliery but was always destined to join the railway. His father, Billy, a porter at Heath station (he just might be one of those figures on the down platform in the previous view), had brought his young family to live at no. 5, Railway Cottages, just behind Heath's up platform, and Herbert's two brothers, Bill and David, were also on the Great Central, as platelayers. Herbert strengthened the railway connection even more in 1928, when he married Hannah from no. 1, Railway Cottages. Hannah's father was Harry Gibson, signalman at Heath Junction, and her Uncle Charlie was a signalman at

Duckmanton North Junction, while her brother Tom was a subganger, one rank up from platelayer. It was almost a family business !

Right: Herbert stayed at Heath until 1925, when he began his long association with Chesterfield Central. Here we see him with a friend by Heath station's entrance in 1923 or, at the latest, 1924. The Railway Clearing House's notice warns of a possible ASLEF strike, which transpired in January, 1924, and it will be noted that the poster board is still headed "Great Central Railway" though Herbert's cap badge is an LNER monogram – this must be immediately post-grouping. Heath station's main (down platform) station building was destroyed, understood to be by a disastrous fire, and had to be replaced, but precisely *when* has yet to be established. The partially visible entrance beneath its arc toplight and within a horizontally boarded structure are typically 'Derbyshire Lines' and definitely not the mock-Tudor replacement, so the fire cannot have been before 1923, at the very earliest. Certainly not 1916 which is generally accepted and was repeated in Derbyshire Lines Part One. The things Herbert told me, but then again the things that I wish I could go back and ask him now.

The southward view from the road bridge, after the replacement by a hipped roof, mock-Tudor station building on the down platform. The umbrella awnings over both platforms are equally atypical and arguably don't fit very comfortably on the original up platform buildings. The line in the left hand corner, passing behind the station 'box, leads to Hardwick Colliery (more commonly known as Holmewood) and its coke ovens dating from 1910, which loom in the left distance. The coke ovens closed in 1962, the colliery following five years later. The pit village of Holmewood grew around Heath station after the line opened. The prominent mock-Tudor gabled building directly opposite the station was the Holmewood Hotel before, like so many establishments of its type, it closed and has latterly been converted for commercial use. Was one the inspiration for the other ?   ***Douglas Thompson***

Leicester Central shed's B1 no. 61188, brand new from Vulcan Foundry in July, 1947, still in LNER green with her LNER no. 1188 on July 19th, 1948, hurrying through Heath with the 12.30 pm Manchester London Road to Leicester Central.   *W.A.Camwell/E.M.Johnson collection*

And here she is again, in more familiar BR guise and by January 2nd, 1960 a Colwick engine, more modestly employed on the 10.09 Sheffield Victoria to Nottingham Victoria 'stopper'. She will remain at Colwick until the end of her career in November, 1965.   *R.J.Buckley/Initial Photographics*

Annesley's typically scruffy O1 no. 63650 heads for home with an interminable string of empties from Heath in the mid-fifties. The rear of her train is still out of sight, snaking out of the Williamthorpe branch sidings. No. 63650 is another old soldier, Kitson's ROD no. 1609 of March, 1918, which went to France the following month. She was loaned to the Great Central on her return, but then mouldered at Morecambe from August, 1921 until she was one of that last batch purchased for virtually nothing by the LNER in February, 1927. Unsurprisingly she wasn't fit for traffic until May, 1929 Rebuilt in May, 1945 she was one of Annesley's stud of O1s until their dispersal, going first to March then coming back to home territory at Staveley in February, 1960. She and Staveley shed bowed out together, in June 1965.

Ken Plant

Heath station closed, along with all the other Derbyshire Lines stations, in March, 1963, but despite the loss of the footbridge and the uprooted running in board lying on the platform, it is still essentially intact over three years later as one of the last York – Bournemouth expresses hurries through, headed by a Darnall English Electric type 3, as we used to know the 37s. The York – Bournemouth was the last bastion of the Great Central main line expresses, a reminder of the Great Central's so very useful cross-country services, which ran until the very end in September, 1966.

Bob Tebb

The last York – Bournemouth has gone, the tracks are gone and so have the platform coping stones. Heath station remains, remarkably unvandalised, its boarded up frontage contrasting with the original up side building, displaying a striking similarity to the Holmewood Hotel over the road. There was no other station like it. The 'H' section girder constructed canopy supports are a poor substitute for the cast columns seen at other Derbyshire Lines stations. Could it have been that the original didn't have the standard ridge and furrow canopies after all ? *Author*

With Homewood's coke ovens in the background, and the colliery headstocks just visible to their right, Staveley's O4/3 no. 63701 is bringing another through haul of coal past Holmwood (sic) Colliery signal box on September 12th, 1963. She is obviously going well, with a white feather above her safety valves, but the gradient post signifies that she has topped the 1-in-100, the remaining mile and a half-or-so to Pilsley summit is an easier 1-in-300. The goods loop was obviously installed after the initial building of the line, necessitating some excavation of the cutting side behind a low retaining wall. No. 63701 is another of the LNER's legion of ex-ROD's – what a bargain they were. Originally ROD no. 1684, by Robert Stephenson's in July 1918, she was demobbed to a loan spell on the Great Eastern before being rescued by the LNER from the Aintree dump in February, 1925. She will remain a Staveley engine until the shed closes in June 1965 but will then only last until that August at Langwith Junction. *Bob Tebb*

On September 29th, 1959, B1 no. 61370 passed the same spot, having an easy day out with an inspection saloon – and a very sumptuous carriage it looks too – though quite what was being inspected must be left to conjecture. The arches over the line beyond the up goods loop turnouts indicate the whereabouts of the girder bridge beneath which the former Midland Railway's Hardwick Colliery branch crosses at a quite an acute angle, heading for a junction with the Pilsley Extension. The loop was a late LNER addition, entailing slicing into the cutting side behind a low retaining wall. Only outshopped by North British Loco's Queen's Park Works in October, 1950, no. 61370 had taken the number of a Robinson Great Central class 9Q (LNER B7) 4-cylinder 4-6-0, GC no. 462, withdrawn in November, 1948. The new no. 61370 was a Sheffield Darnall engine at this time, but included allocations to former Great Northern and Great Eastern sheds in a career still short of 15 years when she was withdrawn from Frodingham in July, 1965. *Michael Mensing*

"Holmwood" Colliery signal box, after closure, in 1967. The railways were ever idiosyncratic with their spelling. The earlier photographs were taken from the Chesterfield – Tibshelf road bridge seen in the background; because of its peculiar acoustics known to locals as the "whistling bridge". It will be noted that the up loop has survived the lifting of the main lines. Accessed via the former Midland branch, it was retained as a headshunt until Holmewood Colliery closed.

Syd Hancock/Graham Perrin

In happier days, a truly unique event saw the preserved Great Western 4-4-0 no. 3440 *City of Truro* heading north along the Great Central in 1959. No wonder the signalman has come to his door for a better look. That September, in even less familiar territory, she would be partnering *Gordon Highlander* and *Glen Douglas*, together with the Highland Jones Goods and the Caley Single working specials in conjunction with the Scottish Industries Exhibition then being held in Glasgow. It was obviously a quite beautiful day, something for which the photographer would have been grateful – he had waited 4 hours to capture this shot.

Bob Tebb

The September 29th, 1959 view from the other side of the Tibshelf road bridge, as V2 no. 60981 hurried by with an up fitted. The leading vehicle is a cattle van, now as much a part of railway history as is the Great Central line itself. The wagons in the far distance are on the Midland's Pilsley Extension line, converging from the west. No. 60981 was built at Darlington in April, 1944. Apart from a few months in 1953 she will be a York North engine throughout her career, until April 1963.

Michael Mensing

She was followed about 40 minutes later by Colwick 'Jazzer' K3 no. 61974, accelerating away from the Heath stop with the 10.09 am Sheffield Victoria – Nottingham Victoria 'all stations'. Isn't the Gresley brake a delight ? No. 61974 was built at Darlington in November, 1936 and will be withdrawn from Immingham in July 1962, just one of the many withdrawals which will have the class extinct by the end of the year. It went largely unnoticed at the time what a year of carnage for British Railways' steam locomotives 1962 was. *Michael Mensing*

Heading on past the goods loop, with Holmewood's coke ovens silhouetted in the background, Mexborough's WD no. 90582 has a change from the usual mineral wagons as her up class H load. Built at Vulcan Foundry as WD no. 77127 (briefly 7127), no. 90582 will remain a 'Mexborough Pacific' until withdrawal in March, 1964, meeting her end shortly afterwards, just along the line at Thomas Ward's Beighton yard. *Syd Hancock*

In the summer of 1963, 'Jubilee' 45646 *Napier* sweeps by the same spot with the Bradford – Poole. Built at Crewe in December, 1934, *Napier* is, as will be expected, a Farnley Junction engine and will remain so until she is withdrawn in December of 1963. ***Syd Hancock***

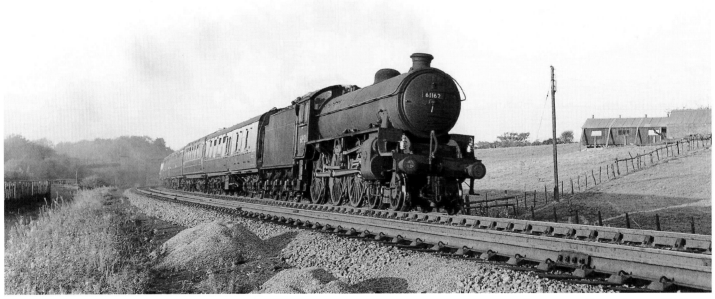

Michael Mensing made invaluable use of his one and only visit to the Derbyshire Lines, not least in capturing Darnall B1 no. 61162 sweeping past Highhouse farm, within a mile of Pilsley station, with the 4.05 pm Manchester London Road – Marylebone express. Built at Vulcan Foundry in May, 1947, no. 61162 will be withdrawn from New England in December, 1964. The line coming from beneath the bridge in the background is the former Midland Railway's Pilsley extension, which was first in the field here. One of the maze of lines which once criss-crossed the coalfield, providing many collieries with two rail connections - three when the Great Northern could get in on the act - the Pilsley extension wandered from Wingerworth, on the Midland main line south of Chesterfield, tapping collieries along the way, before effecting a junction with the Midland's own Pilsley colliery branch. The Midland's Hardwick colliery branch has trailed in just beyond the bridge. Today, the occasional stretch of embankment or isolated length of cutting are all that remains to remind us of these lines, but in this area there is nothing. All traces of both the railway and the coal industry it once served have been erased in an admirable reversion to a natural landscape. Its almost as if the Industrial Revolution had never happened. ***Michael Mensing***

Looking quite tidy, for a WD, and with steam to spare, 'Mexborough Pacific' no. 90190 brings an up mixed goods out of the shadows of Broomridding wood. The Midland's Pilsley extension and the MS&L/GC ran side-by-side as far as Pilsley station but without making a physical connection. No. 90190 was built by North British Loco in September, 1943, originally as WD no. 7218 – then 77218. She will last until February, 1966. *Michael Mensing*

Looking in the opposite direction, Woodford's B1 no. 61078 has just crossed the Locko Lane viaduct with the Bournemouth West – Newcastle, over six hours on from its 11.16 am departure. She will have taken over from a Western Region engine (probably a Hall) at Woodford and will hand over to a York engine (maybe a B16) at Sheffield Victoria, at about 6 o'clock. No. 61078 (North British, September 1946) will remain at Woodford Halse to see out her career in October, 1962. Part of Moorhouse Farm is visible on the left but Pilsley Colliery, on the right, has already been closed for two-and-a-half years. Pilsley was an old colliery, producing coal since 1866, which had initially been served by the Midland Railway's 2½ mile branch from Doe Hill on the Erewash Valley line. It was subsequently given northern access by the Pilsley extension, via Williamthorpe and Grassmoor to Avenue Sidings, Wingerworth, Chesterfield, but that had been severed at Locko Lane long before closure of the colliery. By 1900 production had reached 1200 tons per day, but the colliery closed on April 27th, 1957, making Pilsley a mining community which no longer had a reason for being. It would be joined by many more over the ensuing decades. *Michael Mensing*

The Bournemouth – Newcastle is followed by Staveley's O4/3 no. 63845, heading for home with coal empties. The higher of the two girder bridges in the distance is a footbridge, the lower carried the Great Central branch into the by now closed Pilsley Colliery, partly masked by its spoil heaps. Those spoil heaps are now unrecognisable as the Locko Plantation, a landscaped woodland which rings with birdsong. No. 63845 was yet another of the LNER's ex-RODs, no. 2043, though too late for overseas service when built by the North British Hyde Park Works in May 1919. A spell on loan to the Great Central preceded a long wait at Morecambe before she was part of the final job lot picked up by the LNER in February, 1927, but not made fit for service until March, 1928. Her career will end, still a Staveley engine, in June 1961.

Michael Mensing

The MS&L Derbyshire Lines did not feature soaring viaducts, the nearest approximation being the distinctly functional Locko Lane viaduct, opposite Pilsley colliery's slag heaps, here being crossed by an up goods train behind an unidentified 'Dub-Dee'. Along with the infilling of the cuttings and levelling of the embankments, Locko Lane viaduct has been swept away, its former whereabouts just indicated by a dip in the 'Five Pits Trail', which more or less follows the "returned to nature" route of the Great Central railway.

Bob Tebb

A more oblique view of Locko Lane viaduct with another up goods, but considerably less ordinarily being headed by a Stanier 'Black 5'. In the Great Central main line's final days, Annesley did its best to run the Nottingham Victoria – Marylebone semi-fasts with Black 5s – has one of those been borrowed to bring coal from Williamthorpe or Holmewood ? Moorhouse farm is visible on the skyline to the right, Broomridding wood to the left. ***Bob Tebb***

B1 no. 61186 is hurrying south, light engine, her single lamp tells us, though the pier of bridge no. 53 would have hidden whatever stock might have been coupled behind her tender. The Great Central's Pilsley colliery branch has climbed from beside Pilsley station and is now crossing over bridge 53 to reach the colliery, to our left. The wagons just visible under the left hand span of the bridge are at the southern end of the Midland's severed Pilsley extension, now at a higher level than the Great Central and just north of the junction with the Midland's colliery branch proper. The further bridge, barely visible through no. 61186's exhaust, serves a footpath between Upper Pilsley and Hardstoft. No. 61186 was built at Vulcan Foundry in July, 1947. She will only last until November, 1962. ***Bill Hudson***

PILSLEY

With Pilsley Colliery on the skyline, Colwick 'Jazzer' no. 61870 dashes through Pilsley station with an up special, on July 23rd, 1955. Built at Doncaster in April, 1929, no. 61870 will pitch and lurch no longer after July, 1962, the year of K3 Armageddon. The GC's colliery branch can be seen climbing from behind the up platform. That white-on-black "T" 'Termination of Temporary Speed Restriction' indicator beyond the down platform might indicate permanent way working behind us, or more probably marks the end of a restriction resulting from mining subsidence, which is also the likely explanation for the low platforms.

Henry Priestley

Pilsley station, looking south, with the station signal box visible through the bridge. In an earlier age, when the extinction of the coal industry would have been unthinkable, Pilsley opened with the commencement of passenger services over the line, on January 2nd, 1893. It was a slightly scaled down version of the overbridge booking hall type already seen at Chesterfield, Staveley and Renishaw, with the platform buildings perfectly matched by their glazed ridge and furrow canopies. For the size of the village, the station facilities were lavish. The tall distant signal looking rather incongruous out to the right was nothing to do with the Great Central. It stands sentinel over the Midland Railway's Pilsley colliery branch, alongside just here but about to veer away to the west, under Station Road and on to a junction with the Midland's Erewash Valley line, just north of Doe Hill at Morton sidings.

Lens of Sutton

Pilsley station's booking hall, facing on to Station Road, in its earliest days before advertisements or even notice boards had been affixed. Pilsley station was on the eastern edge of the village, which is to the left, with Station Road pointing towards the neighbouring village of Hardstoft, about a mile to the right. Today a motorist could drive straight past this spot without realising that there had ever been a station, or indeed a railway. *Lens of Sutton*

The southward view again, this time from the up platform in 1951, as an unidentified O1 rattles through with an unfitted express freight, her lamps say. The station is still largely in original condition apart from the loss of its platform canopies – dismantled to save the cost of the constant maintenance battle with subsidence. Just their former cast bracket supports remain. The starter's repeater for sighting will be noted. *Stations UK*

The 1951 view down from the footbridge reveals that only the centre three bays of the platform buildings were enclosed rooms, the end two being open-fronted storage areas, for parcels, etc. The Pilsley colliery branch is clearly visible, climbing away in the right distance before swinging back over the main line.
Stations UK

The final transformation at Plisley was the removal of the platform buildings altogether, and their replacement by simple shelters – a reversal of Renishaw Central, where the overbridge booking hall was dispensed with while the platform buildings survived. The economy measure was insufficient to save the station which closed on November 20th, 1959, over three years before the other Derbyshire Lines stations. Nevertheless the station was still substantially intact, if becoming rather overgrown, when Tinsley's Brush Type 4 – as we then knew Class 47 – no. D1572 hurried through with a 1966 'York - Bournemouth'. Pilsley colliery has been closed even longer, since 1957, but is still evident with its spoil heaps at upper right, though the rusted and overgrown colliery branch, in the right foreground, tells its own story. Built at Crewe in April, 1964, D1572 will ultimately be withdrawn as Class 47 no. 47018 in November, 1991. The two-tone green livery suited them, and didn't it look well when with the York – Bournemouth's Southern green carriages ? *Bob Tebb*

Another post-closure view of the station, on March 2ⁿᵈ, 1963, as 'Jinty' no. 47283 (North British, September 1924) bustles northwards beneath the booking hall. The footbridge with its wooden canopy will be noted, unique on the Derbyshire Lines with steps up into the booking hall, Not a common type on the Great Central, 47283 is in all probability heading for Williamthorpe Colliery to act as BR pilot. She will have reached the Great Central via the New Hucknall colliery branch connection, the improbable route preferred to squeezing the light engine movement on to the very busy Midland main line via Clay Cross and Avenue sidings. No. 47283 needn't look so self-important though; a long time London resident, she only came to Toton in September, 1962 to see out her career and will be withdrawn the following month.

On the 10 o'clock Bradford - Marylebone up express in 1937, former Great Northern class C1 Atlantic no. 4412 bursts out from under Pilsley's Station Road. In the right background, the colliery line is already beginning its climb beneath an upward tilt of the road bridge. The C1s were no strangers to the Great Central, a number having come in exchange for the 'Directors' and 'Lord Faringdons' seconded to the Kings Cross line, and no. 4412 was a Sheffield engine for over twenty years from April, 1924. They were well liked in spite of their comfortless cabs and diabolical riding – which at least ensured an even spread of coal across their wide fireboxes ! Perhaps GC enginemen took some satisfaction from the engines' failure to realise their potential until given high pressure boilers with 32-element Robinson superheaters. No. 4412 (Doncaster, March 1906) is of course carrying her first LNER number, her Great Northern number plus 3000. She will survive to be renumbered 2842 in October, 1946, but only just, withdrawal coming in May, 1947.   ***A Pycock***

Our friend 'Jubilee' no. 45581 *Bihar and Orissa* once again, hurrying a July, 1964 Poole – Bradford by Pilsley station signal box. She is about to pass under the Station Road bridge, which overlooked the Great Central's Pilsley colliery branch junction, though by this time it was already closed and the reception sidings filled with stored wagons. *Mike Eggenton*

TIBSHELF

Pilsley station marked the summit of the Derbyshire Lines: apart from a couple of short rises its now downhill all the way to Annesley and on to Nottingham Victoria. Tibshelf is only a mile and a half or so on from Pilsley and we have caught up again with Michael Mensing on his September 29th, 1959 visit. Here he took up position on a the bridge leading to Church Lane, which runs along the top of the cutting, opposite, just north of the station and overlooked by the parish church of St. John the Baptist. What changes that church has seen: from feudal agricultural beginnings through the growth and demise of a weaving cottage industry and, inevitably, coal mining, from the shallow workings of the 16th Century to the deep mines of the 19th Century, which in their turn became history from 1939. But, arguably, nothing impacted upon Tibshelf more profoundly than the coming of the MS&L Derbyshire Lines. A tunnel had been intended here, but the ground proved too unstable for tunnelling – it kept collapsing – and dictated the excavation of the deep cutting which bisected the village. That, in turn, enforced the construction of the bridge in the background, reconnecting the severed High Street and the "Top" and the "Bottom" ends of the village. Perhaps because of its being an afterthought, uniquely for the Derbyshire Lines, the bridge was of timber – the largest wooden bridge in the country, it was locally said to be. The bridge was replaced by that seen here, in 1951, with massive girders supplied by the Butterley Company. 9F no. 92073 is about to pass under the High Street bridge and through the station (just visible beyond the bridge) with a train of coal for the Annesley yards. After the arrival of the 9F 'Spaceships' at Annesley, no. 92073 in March, 1957, they virtually monopolised the Woodford 'Runners', but they were considerably less common north of Annesley. The magnificent 9Fs had tragically short lives. Not built at Crewe until February, 1956, no. 92073 will be withdrawn in November, 1967.   *Michael Mensing*

No. 92073 is followed a few minutes later by Darnall B1 no. 61111, drifting to a Tibshelf Town stop not far off an hour after her departure from Sheffield Victoria with the 2.17 pm. all stations to Nottingham Victoria. New from North British Loco in December, 1946, no. 61111 will remain a Darnall engine until she is withdrawn in December, 1962. The carriages are of note: an elegant Gresley brake behind a Thompson semi-corridor, a non-gangwayed carriage in which a central pair of lavatories were each accessed by an internal corridor, balanced one on each side as is evident from the door and window arrangement. An ingenious idea for secondary services in those long gone days when passenger comfort was considered to matter.   *Michael Mensing*

A return to the Great Central's latter-day staple traffic as Colwick's WD no. 90703 clanks by with empty iron ore tipplers – can't you just hear the wagons rhythmic rumble over the rail joints ? Vulcan Foundry's WD no. 79263 of February, 1945, no. 90703 will be withdrawn in July 1965, meeting her end the following year at Cox and Danks, of Wadsley Bridge.
Michael Mensing

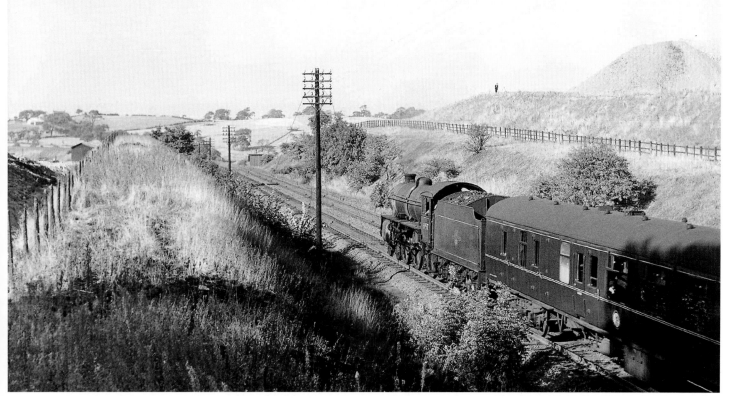

B1 no. 61157 has just passed through Tibshelf, heading back the way we have come with the 12.15 pm Marylebone to Manchester London Road. The otherwise rural landscape features evidence of the opencast workings on either side of the line. Built by Vulcan Foundry in May, 1947, no. 61157 was a Doncaster engine at this time and presumably has been borrowed. Her days will end, still a Doncaster engine, in August 1965.
Michael Mensing

Above: Just a few minutes after no. 61157 passed – their paths would have crossed round about Pilsley station – Leicester shed's uncustomarily immaculate B1 no. 61376 hurries by, an hour and a half after leaving Manchester London Road with the 2.10 pm to Marylebone. No. 61376 wasn't out-shopped by North British until April, 1951, but she will be withdrawn in February 1962 after a career of less than eleven years.

Michael Mensing

Left: As already noted, the 9F 'Spaceships' weren't nearly as common north of Annesley as they were to the south, but no. 92089 has a down mixed goods, mainly comprising coal. Only built at Swindon in September, 1956, no. 92089 will be withdrawn in February, 1967. **Michael Mensing**

Above: One more look southward towards Tibshelf Town, as J11 'Pom-Pom' no. 64444 (GC 9J no. 16, Gorton, April 1909) heads for Annesley, having finished her manoeuvres at Grassmoor, where we met her earlier in the day. Today, the cutting has been filled in, but if anything the resulting green swathe divides the village even more incongruously than did the railway. ***Michael Mensing***

Right: The High Street bridge commanded a fine panorama, with Tibshelf Bottom colliery tip on the skyline and Tibshelf Town station in the foreground. "Tibshelf Town" it always was, though Tibshelf never achieved township status and remains a village to this day. The fence leading up from the sidings behind the up platform marks the line of the "Chicken Run" footpath. Whether by that or the station approach, out of shot to the right, it was a steep climb up to the High Street. Fowler's LMS Class 4s were never commonplace on the Derbyshire Lines, and no. 42361 (Derby, July 1929) had just a year at Annesley from January 1959 before returning to more familiar territory at Trafford Park. In the meantime she is starting away from the Tibshelf stop with the 1.00 pm Leicester Central to Chesterfield Central. Her career though will end on the Great Central, at Gorton in February, 1964. ***Michael Mensing***

Tibshelf Town station in original condition, looking southwards down the "Chicken Run" on a beautiful summer's evening in early BR days. At this time Tibshelf Town was noted for its well-tended gardens, with lupins a particular speciality. This is just as we would like to remember our railways.

Richard Morton collection

Tibshelf Town station from the south, in its latter days. At other Derbyshire Lines stations we have seen how the outer ends of the platform canopies were lightened by bevelling them to a not displeasing hipped effect: at Tibshelf a more severe measure was taken, the main, downside, platform canopy being crudely chopped off beyond the former midpoint support columns. The chimney tops' formerly decorative brickwork has been simplified but the subsidiary up side building was demolished altogether and, as on Pilsley's platforms, replaced by a utilitarian shelter – little more than a prefabricated shed.

Stations UK

Tibshelf Town station in original condition, as it opened on January 2nd, 1893, in the Edwardian era still in the MS&L colour scheme of light and dark stone, later to be superseded by the Great Central's equally attractive two tone green. The station conforms to the Derbyshire Lines 'non-overbridge' style, in which the main station building - in this case on the down platform – is a pitched roof structure with a sawtooth frontage to match the canopy. The subsidiary building, or both platform buildings at overbridge stations, is of the same ridge and furrow profile. Both feature the arc-topped door and window toplights. The original platform will be noted, constructed of wood because the ground was so prone to movement. The platforms were later replaced more substantially but subsidence continued to be a problem throughout the line's existence. ***GCRS collection***

...and here is the subsidiary building in original condition. The five bay ridge and furrow profile in which the outer bays are open-fronted storage areas is typical. ***Lens of Sutton***

Tibshelf Town in an intermediate state. The up platform building is still there, but shorn of its canopy and, as is evident, so is the northernmost bay of the cropped down platform canopy.

Douglas Thompson

The writing on the wall was indeed "writ large" for the Great Central main line on January 2nd, 1960 - the 67th anniversary of Tibshelf Town station's opening - when the very last up 'South Yorkshireman' passed through behind Stanier 'Black 5' no. 45450. She is working back home to Leicester Central after taking over at Sheffield Victoria from a Bradford Low Moor engine. Built by Armstrong Whitworth in December, 1937, no. 45450 will move on from Leicester only the following week, on January 9th, 1960, initially just up the line to Annesley but ultimately to Lostock Hall, where her career will end in November, 1967.

R.J.Buckley

A more prosaic working through Tibshelf on January 2nd, 1960 is 'Mexborough Pacific' no. 90119 (WD no. 77022, North British, March 1943), shouldering along with that typical WD gait at the head of a New Hucknall to Staveley class H goods. She will move on from Mexborough to see out her career at Frodingham in January, 1965. This view from the north end of the station, now in London Midland Region maroon and cream, accentuates the latter day up platform shed but, even so, everything looks fresh and clean, apart from the WD of course.   *R.J.Buckley*

Despite having been closed for two months, Tibshelf Town is still intact on May 9th, 1963, as the steady beat of Staveley's O1 no. 63784 is about to be drowned out by the rhythmic *basso profundo* of her coal wagons, rumbling southward through the station. No. 63784 is another old soldier, ex-ROD no. 1881, from North British's Hyde Park Works in May, 1918. After serving in France, then going on loan to the Great Eastern Railway until recalled to Aintree, she was purchased by the LNER in February, 1925. Rebuilt as an O1 in April, 1945, she is heading for her old stamping grounds at Annesley, where she had worked the Woodford 'Runners' for over six years before being displaced by the arrival of the 9Fs, in 1957. She looks pretty spruce here but has only a couple of months left, until July, 1963.   *John Henton*

Little has changed by June 20th, 1964, when sister engine no. 63868 rattles through Tibshelf Town, with an 'express goods' head code for her iron ore empties, but changes are afoot. The track materials in the foreground are in readiness for the replacement of redundant turnouts by plain track, the goods yard having closed the previous month. Originally North British Loco's Hyde Park Works ROD no. 2081 of August, 1919, no. 63868 was immediately loaned to the Caledonian - one of their 'Froggies' despite, like many of the others, never having been anywhere near France. They were disliked on the Caley for their right-hand drive and there would have been little regret when she was recalled in 1921 to moulder at the Gretna dump until she was one of the last ones picked up for a pittance by the LNER in February, 1927. Rebuilt to class O1 in February, 1945 she will see out her time at Staveley shed until it closes in June 1965. As was so often the case, her transfer to Langwith Junction will be purely nominal, withdrawal coming almost immediately.

Syd Hancock

Looking in the opposite direction, again on June 20th, 1964, the roads and access points of Tibshelf Town's goods yard, dull and pitted from disuse, are apparent as 'Jubilee' no. 45562 *Alberta*, then a Farnley Junction engine, races by with the Poole – Bradford. Built by North British Loco in August, 1934, *Alberta* will move on to Holbeck in December, 1966 to become one of the revered celebrities of steam's final days. What a pity that she did not survive: she was cut up a few months after being withdrawn in November, 1967.

Syd Hancock

A few days earlier, on June 16th, 1964, English Electric Type 3 no. D6799 had swept by the closed Tibshelf Town station with the returning York-Bournemouth; for some reason Bournemouth-York never did sound right, much less Newcastle, did it ? Vulcan Foundry had delivered no. D6799 new to Sheffield in December, 1962, initially at Darnall but, since May, 1964, at Tinsley. She will eventually be withdrawn from Gateshead in June, 1997 but happily will not be scrapped. She lives on in preservation, as Class 37 no. 37324, celebrating in the name *Clydebridge* on the Gloucestershire Warwickshire Railway.

Syd Hancock

The Great Central left Tibshelf heading pretty well due south, passing the adjacent Tibshelf Bottom colliery and the mile or so branch to the Top colliery, immediately before bridging the Midland Railway branch from Westhouses, on the Erewash Valley line, to Mansfield Woodhouse - yet another colliery tapping line, which lost its passenger service as early as 1930. Both Tibshelf collieries closed in the 'thirties, Bottom colliery in 1933, Top colliery in 1939. Once clear of Tibshelf the line curved around to a south-easterly course, skirting the neighbouring village of Newton, where in the autumn of 1963 we meet Staveley's O1 no. 63630 slogging up the 1-in-132 with a down goods. Originally Nasmyth Wilson's ROD no. 1712 of February 1918, no. 63630 had a spell as a Caledonian 'Froggy' (unlike others, she had seen service in France) before being recalled to Gretna in August, 1921, from where she was eventually rescued by the LNER in February, 1927. Rebuilt as an O1 in June, 1945 and between 1951 and 1957 a stalwart of the Annesley – Woodford 'runners', no. 63630 has been at Staveley since January, 1960. She will remain there until the shed closes in June, 1965, to be withdrawn as a Langwith Junction engine.

Syd Hancock

The eastern edge of Newton is on the right skyline in this September, 1959 view of WD no. 90250 (WD no. 77350, North British, August 1943) coasting down the bank with an up local goods, very possibly for New Hucknall sidings. She has just passed under Alfreton Road: the bridge is hardly discernible but the alignment is apparent from the houses and bungalows to the left, and is now about to pass under Cragg Lane which connected Newton with Blackwell, immediately to the south. No. 90250's career will end in March, 1963. *Michael Mensing*

Raven B16 'Bloodspitters' were no strangers to the Great Central line, whether in original condition like York North's no. 61458, or both Gresley and Thompson rebuilds. Genuine mixed traffic engines, they generally only brought passenger trains as far south as Sheffield Victoria from their native north-east, but were frequently to be seen on York – Woodford fast fitteds, as seen here. Built to the North Eastern Railway S3 design, no. 61458 was among those built after the Grouping, emerging from Darlington Works in October, 1923 as LNER no. 1375. Other than one engine destroyed by wartime bombing, the B16s remained intact until 1958, but 61458 is in her final days. She will be withdrawn in November, 1959. *Michael Mensing*

A rather sad sight at Cragg Lane: one-time pride of the West Coast main line, 'Royal Scot' no. 46156 *The South Wales Borderer* reduced to trundling coke hoppers to the Annesley yard. The rebuilding of the 'Scots', commencing in 1942, transformed them, but was nevertheless an unhurried process and there were still a final two waiting their turn when *The South Wales Borderer*, originally built at Derby in July, 1930, was rebuilt in May, 1954. She had only just arrived at Annesley when she was photographed at Cragg Lane on October 25th, 1963 but in truth, by the time they reached Annesley, the hand-me-down 'Scots' were poor, worn out things. She will be withdrawn in October, 1964. **Syd Hancock**

9F No. 92030 (Crewe, November 1954) has passed under Cragg Lane and takes an up goods towards the Huthwaite Lane bridge, in the distance. An Annesley engine since June, 1957, no. 92030 will move on to Banbury and Saltley before being withdrawn from Wakefield in February, 1967. **Michael Mensing**

….. and the southward view from Huthwaite Lane, as Leicester Central's B1 no. 61380 hurries by with the up 'South Yorkshireman' with which she left Sheffield Victoria at 11.30 and is due into Nottingham Victoria at half past twelve - it will be about quarter past now. No. 61380 will take the train as far as Leicester Central, her home shed since February, 1953, from where she took a down working to Sheffield earlier in the day. Her service life will end in March, 1962, just 10½ years after arriving at Colwick from North British Loco in August, 1951.   *Michael Mensing*

Beyond Blackwell the Great Central passed to the north of the village of Hilcote, where in the summer of 1963 we again meet the Poole – Bradford, headed by Farnley Junction 'Jubilee' no. 45646 *Napier* whom we met earlier at Holmewood on the up working.   *Syd Hancock*

On September 3rd, 1966, B1s nos. 61173 and 61131 with the Locomotive Club of Great Britain's valedictory 'Great Central Railtour' are passing the same spot, close by the point where the M1 will soon cross the trackbed. Within days the track here will be ripped up to allow the motorway's construction. Some call it progress. Nos. 61173 and 61131 have brought the 'Great Central Railtour' from Nottingham Victoria where it had arrived from Waterloo behind 'Merchant Navy' no. 35030 *Elder Dempster Lines*. They will take it on via Woodhouse East Junction and the Darnall curve through Wath, before an electric completes the journey from Elsecar to Penistone and back to Sheffield Victoria. The B1s will be waiting there to take the return working by way of the former LD&EC 'Clog and Knocker' to Langwith Junction, regaining the main line at Kirkby South Junction, as far as Nottingham Victoria from where *Elder Dempster Lines* will take the weary excursionists back to Marylebone. What a day, and what would we give to be able to make that journey today? The B1s, both Wakefield engines, were not to survive the line by long: no. 61131 (North British, February 1947), which had also been involved with the RCTS's August 13th,1966 'Great Central Railtour', was withdrawn that December; no. 61173 (Vulcan Foundry, June 1947) lasted until January, 1967.

Syd Hancock

NEW HUCKNALL SIDINGS

Having passed Hilcote, the Great Central again curved southwards, setting course for Kirkby-in-Ashfield. In David Dykes deceptively rural view, looking north from beside the Alfreton – Sutton in Ashfield and Mansfield Road (nowadays the A38 dual carriageway), Huthwaite is just out of shot to the right, with Strawberry Bank, one of the contenders for "highest point in Nottinghamshire", in the distance. The complex through which Staveley's O1 no. 63773 is passing is New Hucknall colliery Sidings which once served the Blackwell and New Hucknall collieries via branches curving away west and east respectively from the northern end of the sidings, and the South Normanton colliery by way of the southward branch seen in the left foreground. The New Hucknall line is marked by the line of wagons in the middle distance, pointing to a junction with the Midland's extension of its Blackwell branch (which has just been bridged by the GC main line) immediately before reaching the colliery. South Normanton colliery had closed as early as 1952 – the site is now unrecognisable as the McArthur Glen retail outlet – and Blackwell followed in 1964, but New Hucknall outlived the railway and indeed kept a short stretch of the Great Central main line in use until it too closed in the early 'eighties. The colliery owed its name to having been sunk in 1877, when Huthwaite was still known by its former name of "Hucknall-under-Huthwaite" or, unofficially, "Dirty Hucknall"! No. 63773 was an original Great Central 8K 'Tiny', no. 1213 by North British Loco in August, 1912. She was rebuilt as an O1 in April, 1946 and selected as the LNER's representative in the 1948 Exchange trials heavy goods category on the Western Region. She acquitted herself particularly well and reputedly was the most economical of the trialists but that will count for nothing when she is withdrawn in October, 1964.

David Dykes

Yet more coal for Annesley, and again with a Staveley O1, no. 63630. In 1963 we thought it would go on forever. No. 63630 was originally Nasmyth Wilson's ROD no. 1712 of February, 1918. After repatriation and a spell as a Caley 'Froggie' she had to wait until February, 1927 at Gretna before she was rescued by the LNER, initially as O4/3 no. 6555. Rebuilt to an O1 in June, 1946 she will continue to serve until July, 1965.

Syd Hancock

Was there anything to choose between the various types of O4 ? By all accounts not a great deal: to quote one old GC line engineman "The 'Tinies' were that good, they couldn't spoil them whatever they tried". It is no coincidence that our succession of coal trains passing through the New Hucknall sidings now features O4/8 no. 63726. Yet another of the LNER's old-soldiers, no. 63726 was originally Robert Stephenson's ROD no. 1737 of October 1919 which, too late for the war, went straight on loan to the North Eastern Railway (a "pneumonia engine", according to the Geordie enginemen, used to their own locomotives' commodious side-window cabs). The LNER's O4/3 no. 6500 after she was picked up from Aintree in February 1925, she acquired a shortened O2-type boiler to become an O4/5 in September 1939 but was again rebuilt to her final 100A-boilered O4/8 form in January 1958. That will see her through to April 1964. In the centre of the picture is the flat-roofed BR Type 15 signal box, rather less stylish than the Great Central one it had replaced.

Chris Ward collection

A rather closer view of New Hucknall Sidings' BR Type 15 signal box, on a dismal June 24th, 1967. The sidings are still in use - though, it would appear, hardly intensively – but they are now accessed via that connection from the ex-Midland New Hucknall colliery branch off the Erewash Valley line, trailing in from the right beyond the Ha-penny bridge by which the Hilcote to Huthwaite footpath crosses the line. The Great Central through lines have already been lifted: they formerly ran along that void directly in front of the signal box. Odd though, isn't it, how derelict track bed never looks sufficient to have accommodated the lines which once occupied it ?

Syd Hancock

Another class H goods threading through the New Hucknall sidings and about to pass under the Alfreton Road, behind Staveley's O4/3 no. 63701. As is evident by her O4/3 classification, no. 63701 also began as a ROD, no. 1684 by Robert Stephenson in July, 1918. After being demobilised and loaned to the Great Eastern, she was recalled and stored at Aintree, from where she was purchased by the LNER in February, 1925. She will be withdrawn in August, 1965.

David Dykes

That is the Alfreton Road bridge, beneath which 'Jubilee' no. 45643 *Rodney* has just brought the July 4th, 1964 Bradford – Poole. The South Normanton colliery line is diverging to the left. Built at Crewe in December, 1934, as will be expected *Rodney* is a Farnley Junction engine but will end her career at Holbeck in January, 1966.

Syd Hancock

Some years after the closure of South Normanton colliery its branchline, swinging away to the west, was still *in situ* and in use for wagon storage as seen from the southern side of the Alfreton Road bridge. It is being passed by a northbound class K goods behind an unidentified O4/8. ***David Dykes***

A less usual sight from the southern side of the Alfreton Road bridge which would have had the local spotters rubbing their eyes on June 27th, 1964, is Peppercorn A1 no. 60125 *Scottish Union* (Doncaster, April 1949, named after the winner of the 1938 St. Leger) not too severely taxed by a down pigeon special returning empty, though one would imagine that with pigeons, loaded or empty would make little difference ! It really is though a derisory load for a class of engine designed to haul 550 ton trains at 60-70 mph on the East Coast main line, or for the first A1 (of three) to achieve an authenticated 'ton'. A1s were rare visitors to the Great Central line and *Scottish Union*'s next journey into GC territory will be for cutting up at Cox and Danks, Wadsley Bridge, after she is withdrawn precisely one week later, on July 4th, 1964. The wagons have gone from the South Normanton line but something is keeping the metals polished. ***Syd Hancock***

KIRKBY BENTINCK

Kirkby Bentinck station signal box was directly opposite the goods yard but the station, immediately to its south, had been closed for over a year when Royal Scot no. 46163 *Civil Service Rifleman* (though without her nameplates, removed before they could be unofficially 'acquired') came by with an 'Ian Allan Rail Tour' special on April 7th, 1964. It was a Locospotters Club Special to Doncaster Works, run between Paddington and Leicester Central by GW Castle no. 7029 *Clun Castle*, then taken on via Nottingham Victoria and Staveley Central by no. 46163, which is now on the return trip. Built at Derby in September, 1930, no. 46163 has been made to look quite presentable externally, but Annesley's Scots were on their last legs and she will only last until that August. The line curving away behind the signal box is to Langton colliery, which stayed open until 1966 but remained a prominent landmark for twenty years after that, and, by doubling back upon itself, Bentinck colliery, which wouldn't close until 2000. The line to the left of the running lines is the headshunt for the Bentinck colliery reception sidings, opening out behind us, and the shininess of all the rails indicate they are still very much in business.

Henry Priestley

Kirkby Bentinck station opened with the January 2nd, 1893 introduction of passenger services from Staveley Town to Annesley (and, via the Great Northern, on to Nottingham). Until it was rechristened by the LNER on March 1st, 1925, the station was named 'Kirkby and Pinxton', and was indeed on the Pinxton (south west) side of Kirkby-in-Ashfield, at the foot of Castle Hill, though Pinxton was still little short of a three mile walk away. Other than the change of name, the station is still in original condition in this circa 1930 view towards Nottingham. The alignment at this point is more easterly than to the south, and the girder bridge beyond the station footbridge serves the Pinxton Road, from which the station and its small goods yard (behind the photographer) was reached by a roadway behind the up platform.

Stations UK

In this latter day view of the station, very noticeably the down platform buildings have been replaced, as at Tibshelf Town, by a basic waiting shelter, and in place of the GC lantern-type platform lamps are shaded globes more akin in style to the Midland's. On the other hand, the remaining up platform canopy has survived more completely than at any other of the Derbyshire Lines stations. It has been cut back somewhat from its original 'platform edge' extent, but still retains its original gabled profile. The houses visible behind the down platform are on the northern fringe of the quaintly named Bentinck Town.

Saturday, August 24th, 1907 was a high day for Kirkby and Pinxton station. One wonders how many people, all in their Sunday best, might have excitedly flocked down to the station for the 9.28 am 'Cheap Excursion' to Hyde Road, to wonder at Belle Vue Zoo's exotic exhibits, be enthralled by the re-enactment of the Duke of Marlborough's triumph in the Battle of Blenheim and goodness knows what else, before eventually setting out for home "after the Fireworks" at 11.35 pm. At what ungodly hour would weary parents have been cajoling their fractious offspring back up Kirkby's Church Hill ? Perhaps that Sunday they might have given the morning service at St. Wilfrid's a miss for once. Still, not a bad day out for three shillings and ninepence (about 18p). In those long ago, pre-David Attenborough days, no doubt the excursionists would have appreciated the help of the illustrations on the reverse of the flier, to identify the animals they were looking at. Perhaps it is significant that even in 1907, pick ups at those stations which wouldn't last until the end of the Derbyshire Lines - Pilsley; Grassmoor; Brimington; Beighton - weren't considered worthwhile, but that the special would pass straight through Killamarsh is rather more surprising.

Kirkby Bentinck's up platform building in its final form, differing from the original only by a trimming back of the canopy. By contrast, at Killamarsh Central the outer ends of the canopy had been bevelled to a hipped profile, and even more drastically, at Tibshelf Town they had been hacked back to the support columns.

Frank Ashley

The down platform building, opposite, looks to be 'as built', apart from the canopy glazing. The five-bay format (in which the outer two are open-fronted storage spaces) is standard for subsidiary platform buildings, but this cannot be very long at all before its 1947/8 replacement by a simple waiting shelter.

Barry Hardwick

The replacement shelter was evident when WD no. 90129 trudged through the station with northbound empties in March, 1952. Looking truly pitiable even by 'Dub-Dee' standards, no. 90129 was North British Loco's WD no. 77032 of April, 1943. She will eventually be withdrawn from Immingham shed in June, 1964 and meet her end just up the line from here, at Thomas Ward's yard at Killamarsh.

Frank Ashley

In the opposite direction, a class H coal train for Annesley yards is uncustomarily headed by York's V2 no. 60975 (Darlington, September 1943). As is evident by the absence of external steam pipes she still has her original 'monobloc' cylinder casting. York V2s were no strangers to the Great Central line but generally would be expected on an express passenger, or at least a fitted goods: presumably no. 60975 has been borrowed to make good a temporary shortage of the O4 or WD eight-coupled more usual for this work. She will be withdrawn, still a York engine, in May, 1964.

Seen from the Pinxton Road bridge, B1 no. 61315 (North British, April 1948) has called at Kirkby Bentinck with a Sheffield Victoria – Nottingham Victoria 'stopper'. Fitted with electric lights (thats a Stone's steam-driven generator beside her smokebox), by B1 standards she will have quite a respectable lifespan at nearly 18 years, but when withdrawn in February, 1966 she will continue to serve as a stationary train heating boiler at Barrow Hill as Departmental no. 32. It was only a stay of execution though, until October 1968. Isn't that Gresley brake behind her tender just delicious ? This view makes clear the local topography. The terraces of Bentinck Town's Mayfield Street, discernible in the left middle distance, indicate the continuation of the downward slope from the higher ground to the right. The sidings behind the down platform serve Bentinck colliery, to the south of the line. Kirkby Bentinck's goods yard is beyond the station on the up side with the goods shed visible above the footbridge. ***Gordon Hepburn/Rail Archive Stephenson***

Snow and steam, made for each other ! Another B1-hauled 'stopper', on February 26th, 1955. Darnall's no. 61041 (North British, April 1946) has called at Kirkby Bentinck with Sheffield Victoria's 2.20 pm all stations to Nottingham Victoria. By then a New England engine she will be withdrawn in April 1964. Some of us really should have taken more notice of carriages, such as that choice articulated pair behind 61041's tender. ***Henry Priestley***

On the same day 'Mexborough Pacific' no. 90410 (WD no. 78537, North British 1945) is putting up a voluminous exhaust as she powers through Kirkby Bentinck on a down goods. She will be withdrawn in April 1966 but in the meantime offers proof that, given the right conditions, beauty can be found in the most improbable circumstances. Snow and steam !

Henry Priestley

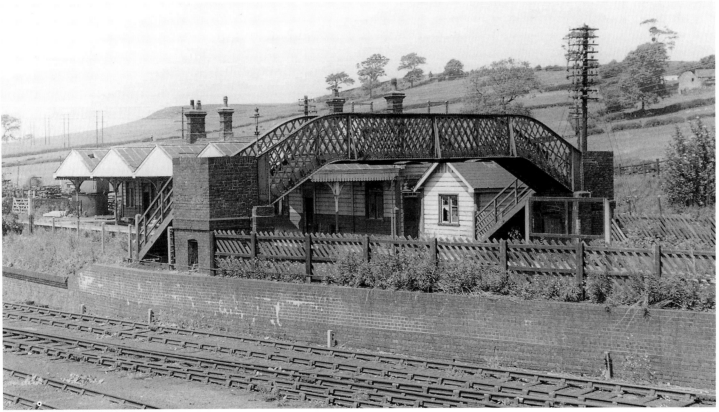

Looking more or less northwards across the Bentinck Colliery reception sidings, the scene appears pleasantly rural, but closer examination reveals that this view post-dates the withdrawal of the Derbyshire Lines locals: the station is closed. Broken windows, the general dereliction along the platform and the empty frame from which the "Kirkby Bentinck" running-in board has been removed, all tell their own story.

Sheffield Darnall's B1 no. 61312 about to pass through Kirkby Bentinck station in 1952, heading for home with a down express. The one-time Kirkby North Junction Signal Box – long since redundant for its original function – is peeping out from behind the Pinxton Road bridge abutment where it was resited from its original position a couple of hundred yards further south. The lattice girder footbridge, visible beside 61312's smokebox, gives access to Mill Lane, heading down the hillside from Kirkby to Bentinck colliery. Shortly beyond, the former Kirkby North to East Junction line diverged to the left. The Great Northern had planned to drive an Annesley tunnel of its own, to gain access to the collieries northwards from Kirkby, but with the MS&L trading running powers over the Derbyshire Lines in return for MS&L powers over the GN into Nottingham, was happy to take advantage of the MS&L tunnel. In the meantime the Great Northern reached the Kirkby Summit Colliery via the North Junction – albeit with a reversal – in 1896. That route was though very short-lived. By 1898 the line from Kirkby South Junction (completing a triangle at Kirkby East Junction) catered for the natural southward traffic flow without the need for a reversal. With but one scheduled trip working (from the GC) by the time of the Great Northern's 1901 working timetable, there was little subsequent requirement for the Kirkby North to East Junctions link and it closed in 1905. Kirkby North Junction signal box followed in 1918 but, as noted, was resited here for use by the Signal and Telegraph department - the railways were into recycling long before it became 'politically correct' ! The Kirkby junctions though can be confusing. The North and South junctions were more or less west and east of each other, while the East Junction was north of both ! The line on the right, which falls away beyond the Mill Lane bridge, leads to the headshunt for Bentinck colliery, on the south side of the line and at a lower level. Bentinck colliery commenced production in 1896 and was notable for being the first British colliery to produce a million tons of coal in seven months. Remaining open until 2000 the colliery considerably outlived the Derbyshire Lines, including by the 1980s processing coal from the by then linked Annesley and Newstead collieries. New to Darnall from North British Loco in April, 1948, no. 61312 will spend much of the later 'fifties in Great Eastern territory before returning to end her days again on Great Central metals, at Mexborough in March, 1964. *Frank Ashley*

With the Mill Lane footbridge in the background, Tinsley's Brush Type 4 no. D1706 in the original two-tone green livery sweeps by the Bentinck colliery empties line and Laburnum Avenue's house backs with a latter-day York – Bournemouth. Being at a significantly lower level than the main line, the colliery was quite awkward to reach. The empties line eased down into a headshunt, which gave kick-back access into a further descent to the colliery, where it shared a common access with a branch off the Midland's line from Pye Bridge. D1706 was at the time a Class 48, one of just five with an experimental engine which proved to be unreliable: they were subsequently re-engined as standard Class 47s. As no. 47118 she will be withdrawn in March, 1991. *John Hitchens*

We're back at our footbridge vantage point for the Bournemouth – York return working, again headed by a Brush Type 4, with the inclination of the Bentinck colliery line evident on the right. The locomotive has just passed the site of Kirkby North Junction, the line from which veered away above the leading carriage. On a clearer day the Great Central's Mansfield line would have been visible converging from the left. *John Hitchens*

Again we are looking southwards, to where an 08 is sandwiched in a considerable rake of empties on the somewhat overgrown colliery line. Above and to the left are first, the Great Central main line, then at a higher level still the Mansfield line. In the distance both are bridging the Midland's Pye Bridge to Kirkby line, which skirts Studfold Wood on the skyline. The Mansfield line bridge is visible above the far end wagons but the main line bridge, to its right, is barely discernible. *John Hitchens*

KIRKBY SOUTH JUNCTION

In this September, 1955 view, the 'Whitland Fish' which we first encountered at Duckmanton South Junction is just passing over the Midland Pye Bridge line. The non-use by this train of the Duckmanton South Junction short cut, provided primarilly for fish traffic, has already been discussed, also that the junction had been largely superseded for that purpose by the Mansfield line, here descending on the right to join the main line at Kirkby South Junction, which carried a considerable traffic in fish – but again, for whatever reason, not the New Clee – Banbury 'Whitland Fish' ! As explained earlier the unidentified train engine 'Jazzer' will be an Immingham engine, but her sister-engine pilot, no. 61980 (originally LNER no. 3820, Darlington, December 1936) is working home to Annesley and will come off at the Nottingham Victoria inspection stop. She will be one of the very last K3s in service when she is withdrawn from Ardsley in December, 1962. With some "smoothing" of the sharp curves to utilise the old Mansfield and Pinxton Railway, the Midland Railway branch from Pye Bridge on the Erewash Valley line dated from as early as 1851, by the 1870s paralleled by the Great Northern's Pinxton branch. After originally connecting at Kirkby Summit, the Midland branch was diverted in the 1890s to join its 1848 line from Nottingham immediately south of Kirkby East station. The Midland line from Nottingham was again from 1881 accompanied cheek by jowl by the Great Northern Leen Valley line, before continuing to Mansfield and, ultimately, to Worksop on the MS&L, via Shireoaks East Junction.   *Frank Ashley*

Seen from within a few yards of the same viewpoint, with the spire of Kirkby-in-Ashfield's St. Wilfrid's hazily behind her, O4/8 no. 63717 is easing coal from the resleepered Mansfield line over the Midland and down to join the main line at Kirkby South Junction. No. 63717 is another ex-ROD, no. 1697 built by Robert Stephenson in March 1919, too late for overseas service and initially loaned to the Great Western, their no. 3021, before being acquired by the LNER in December, 1923. Her March, 1958 rebuild to the final O4/8 form, as seen here, can only have been very recent. She will be withdrawn in April, 1965.   ***Richard Morton collection***

It looks to be about the same time, maybe the same day, judging by the obviously newly reballasted down Mansfield line. Her tender full of slack, B1 no. 61285 (North British, March 1949) is the somewhat improbable motive power for southbound iron ore empties on the main line. On the Great Central, B1s typically worked passenger trains, or at least fitted goods, and an eight-coupled would normally be expected on such a working as this. Colwick was no. 61285's final shed: she will be withdrawn in December, 1965.   ***Richard Morton collection***

Track maintenance under way at the divergence of the Mansfield line at Kirkby South Junction in June, 1953, with Colwick J6 no. 64212 on the PW train. Hard hats ? High-visibility vests ? Whats wrong with cloth caps and dungarees ? Kirkby South Junction Signal Box opened with the Great Northern's Leen Valley Extension line in April, 1898, which ultimately reached up through Sutton-in-Ashfield and Shirebrook to a junction with the Great Central's ex-Lancashire, Derbyshire and East Coast line at Langwith Junction. The Great Northern line diverged immediately beyond the signal box and is hidden within its own rock cutting. The Great Central's Mansfield line was added from 4th September, 1916 - 2nd April, 1917 for passengers, when Kirkby Central station opened. With the Midland already established at Kirkby East there were then three parallel north-south lines through Kirkby, though the Great Northern did not have a passenger station – perhaps an inter-railway politics 'deal' over the GN's use of Annesley Tunnel ? Ironic then that the 1990s resurrected Nottingham-Worksop 'Robin Hood Line', for the most part following the former Midland route, utilises the BR 1972 deviation onto the Great Northern alignment through Kirkby, with a passenger station on the line that never had been one ! No. 64212 (Doncaster, August 1913) originated as Harry Ivatt's Great Northern class J22 no. 1398. Apart from only brief intervals elsewhere, her whole career was spent at Colwick, where a sizeable stud of J6s filled a useful general purpose role. When the withdrawal of J6s began though, in August 1955, she was amongst the earliest to go, that December.   ***Frank Ashley***

The York – Bournemouth will have gone on its way as double-chimney 9F no. 92200 (Swindon, November 1958) brings a rake of 21 ton hoppers snaking off the Mansfield line, the brake van behind the tender strongly hinting at the working. It is one of the last regular workings over the Mansfield line, the Mansfield Concentration Sidings to Kirkby Bentinck empties. It was due shortly after the York – Bournemouth, which it followed as far as the Annesley tunnel mouth where the engine uncoupled and ran light through the tunnel to cross over at Annesley North Junction. It then ran back along the down line to utilise another crossover under our Lindley's Lane bridge vantage point and draw its train back to Kirkby Bentinck. The 30 mph speed limit applicable to the GN turn-off looks likely to be yellow, as distinct from the pre-1963 white, but its hard to be sure. No. 92200 will be withdrawn from Langwith Junction in October, 1965 and soon reduced to scrap just along the line at Wards, Killamarsh. A working life of less than seven years: what a waste.

Richard Morton collection

Slide-valve J11 'Pom-Pom' no. 64336 has brought her stopper just past the Mansfield line turnouts, but with her being a long-term Staveley resident we can assume she has come along the main line. 'Pom-Poms' weren't common though on Sheffield-Nottingham locals, which were more usually five coaches long – lavish accommodation considering what passengers are shoe-horned into nowadays. No. 64336 began life as John G. Robinson's Great Central class 9J no. 211, built by Beyer Peacock in October, 1903. She will meet her end just across the tracks, at Gorton Works in July, 1959.   ***Frank Ashley***

More common fare on the Sheffield Victoria – Nottingham Victoria locals, certainly by 1959, is represented by Darnall's D11 'Director' no. 62661 *Gerard Powys Dewhurst* – a delicious name even if, at the time, we hadn't a clue who that gentleman was ! Originally John G. Robinson's Great Central class 11F no. 507, *Gerard Powys Dewhurst* emerged from Gorton Works in February, 1920. Actually the 11Fs were 'Improved Directors', the true 'Directors' were the earlier 11E (D10) class which had all gone by the mid-50s. By the time of the 11F's arrival, there were only two Great Central directors still to have locomotives named in their honour and nos. 506 (*Butler-Henderson*) and 507 were named accordingly, the remainder of the class bearing the names of members of the Royal Family or Great War battles. No. 62665 *Mons* was the first D11 to be withdrawn, just a month before *Gerard Powys Dewhurst* was photographed on her local on June 20th, 1959. All would disappear though by the end of 1960, *Gerard Powys Dewhurst* in November.

Howard Turner

Another look at the 'Whitland Fish' in June 1956, this time with Annesley B1 no. 61209 (North British, July 1947) getting a lift home as pilot to an anonymous Immingham K3 'Jazzer'. No. 61209 will end her days at Colwick in September, 1962. It will be noted that, unlike the cutting north of the junction, no retaining wall is necessary here to reinforce the sheer-sided magnesian limestone cutting. *Frank Ashley*

A final look back at Kirkby South Junction as Brush Type 4 no. D1572, whom we met earlier at Pilsley, chunters over Kirkby South Junction with the York - Bournemouth. ***Bob Tebb***

The preceding views of Kirkby South Junction are from the bridge on Lindley's Lane, which runs directly southwards from Kirkby. The crossover by which no. 92200 was able to rejoin her Mansfield Concentration Sidings – Kirkby Bentick empties is just visible at the bottom of the picture as we look in the opposite direction in September, 1955. Colwick J39 no. 64757 (Darlington, September 1928) has just emerged from Annesley Tunnel with a local from Nottingham Victoria which the bracket signal indicates is for the former Great Northern Leen Valley Extension line to Sutton-in-Ashfield. The right hand board is for the main line, that in the centre for Mansfield. The Nottingham Victoria – Sutton-in-Ashfield service ceased at the end of 1955, but there was such uproar in Sutton, the loss also of the Central station leaving just the inconveniently sited Midland line station re-maining, that it was reinstated in February, 1956. It was to no avail: the service was withdrawn for good at the end of the Summer Timetable. The Midland's Leen Valley line has burrowed through the Robin Hood Hills at a higher level by its own considerably shorter Kirkby Tunnel and has crossed over the GC tunnel just beyond its portal to head north through Kirkby East station. The resurrected Robin Hood line utilises the former Midland tunnel but then more or less follows the Kirkby South Junction / Great Northern align-ment, though at a considerably higher level. Ironically there is again a bridge here, but Lind-ley's Lane now goes <u>under</u> the railway. No. 64757 will be withdrawn in November, 1962. Its hard to imagine that the cumbersome J39s - 'Standards' to Great Central enginemen – came from the same drawing boards as Gresley's sleek Pacifics and V2s. *Frank Ashley*

Smoke billows out of the Annesley Tunnel behind O4/1 no. 63671, heading for the Mansfield line with coal empties. No. 63671 is an original class 8K 'Tiny', John G. Robinson's Great Central no. 406, built at Gorton in May, 1912. She will be withdrawn in June, 1965. ***Richard Morton collection***

A contrast in bridges. Great Central Bridge no. 83 is the Lindley's Lane bridge we have just left, at the top of the picture with Kirkby South Junction's turnouts just visible through the arch. "Bridge" no. 85 is the Annesley Tunnel from above which we are now looking back along the line. The intervening Bridge no. 84 is the modest structure which Leicester's B1 no. 61128 has just come under, heading for home with an up express. It is an aqueduct for an occasional stream, which flows only in wet weather: 'Runs as required', in railway parlance. No. 61128 was built by North British in February, 1947. She will last only until December, 1962. We didn't realise at the time what a year of steam locomotive carnage 1962 was. ***Jack Cupit***

After the London Midland region's takeover of the Great Central line in 1958, and Leicester shed's loss of its A3s, the Great Central line suffered something of an express passenger locomotive crisis. The problem would shortly be circumvented by the London Midland region getting rid of the expresses altogether, but in the meantime it was at least partially resolved by Annesley's rostering of 9F 'Spaceships' which explains why, on July 29th, 1959, 9F no. 92069 is about to enter Annesley Tunnel with the up 'South Yorkshireman'. No. 92069, built at Crewe in December 1955, was an Annesley engine from February 1957 to May, 1965. She will be withdrawn in May, 1968.
Jack Cupit

The York – Bournemouth again - it kept the Great Central's express train flag flying right to the end - on a day when one would not expect the aqueduct to be "in water", as the canal types put it. The locomotive power is this time being provided by an English Electric Type 3, later to be designated Class 37, but she will be throttling back: Annesley North Junction's distant is 'on' and she must be prepared to stop at the other end of the tunnel. The shallowness of the cutting dates only from the early 'fifties, when increasing ground instability required the sloping back of the cutting, originally steep sided all the way to the tunnel mouth.
John Hitchens

Farnley Junction 'Jubilee' no. 45643 *Rodney*, whom we met at at New Hucknall sidings with the July 4th, 1964 Bradford – Poole, erupts from the northern portal of Annesley tunnel with the same day's Poole – Bradford return.

Syd Hancock

Annesley tunnel's north portal, with the south end visible 997, 1,000 or 1,001 yards away, depending on which authority you believe. It had rarely been possible to see through the generally smoke-filled tunnel other than perhaps on Summer Sunday evenings, but now the dull metals tell their own story: this is after closure. The catch points on the down line will be noted: they are insurance against runaways rolling back through the tunnel on the 1-in-132 falling gradient which has now commenced and, with only a brief derruption through Bulwell Common, will be more or less continuous right through to Nottingham Victoria, which is where we will be going next...

P.C.H. Robinson